PERSPECTIVES ON EARLY
CHILDHOOD EDUCATION:
CONTEMPORARY RESEARCH

PERSPECTIVES ON EARLY CHILDHOOD EDUCATION:
CONTEMPORARY RESEARCH

Edited by Kath Hirst and
Cathy Nutbrown

Trentham Books
Stoke on Trent, UK and Sterling, USA

Trentham Books Limited
Westview House   22883 Quicksilver Drive
734 London Road   Sterling
Oakhill   VA 20166-2012
Stoke on Trent   USA
Staffordshire
England ST4 5NP

First published 2005

British Library Cataloguing-in-Publication Data
A catalogue record for this book is available from the British Library

ISBN-13: 978-1-85856-328-2
ISBN-10: 1-85856-328-3

*The cover picture is taken from Karen Boardman's case study on
using children's drawings for teaching and learning with three to
five year olds (chapter 11).*

Designed and typeset by Trentham Print Design Ltd, Chester and
printed in Great Britain by The Cromwell Press Ltd, Trowbridge.

CONTENTS

DEDICATION

This book is dedicated to those who have only just begun, especially Lola, Charlie, Beth, George, Sophie, Mark, Bethany, Sam, Emily, Christopher, Maiya, Joseph, Jaimie, Tom, Harry, Oliver, Zak, Jack, Jake, Josh, Alfie, Mary, Katherine, James, Adam, Ellie, Abbie, Matthew and Emma Louise

... and in memory of Ian Jenkinson, a wonderful teacher and very special friend. With deep gratitude.

ACKNOWLEDGEMENTS

We should like to thank our colleagues Peter Clough, Peter Hannon, Jackie Marsh and Rachel Watson for their involvement and support at various stages in the compilation of this collection. Particular thanks are due to the contributors to this collection and to Lesley Abbott, Tricia David and Peter Elfer. Finally, our thanks to Gillian Klein and the team at Trentham.

About the editors and contributors

Editors

Dr Kath Hirst is currently teaching on the MA in Early Childhood Education at the University of Sheffield. She has previously worked as a nursery and infant teacher, and advisory teacher. Her research interests include early literacy, family literacy, community provision, and work with parents. Recent research includes the bilingual aspect of the REAL (*Raising Early Achievement in Literacy*) project and evaluation (*Shared Beginnings* and *Early Start*). Her publications are in the field of bilingualism, early literacy and work with parents.

Dr Cathy Nutbrown has an international reputation for her research in early education. She is author of numerous publications in the field of early childhood education. Publications include: *Threads of Thinking* (Sage 1999); *Experiencing Reggio Emilia* (Abbott and Nutbrown 2001); *Respectful Educators – Capable Learners* (PCP 1996) and *A student's Guide to Methodology* (Clough and Nutbrown Sage 2002). Her current research includes the REAL (*Raising Early Achievement in Literacy*) Project (Sage, 2005) and a study of pre-school educators' perspectives on working inclusion in the early years (the CAPE: SEN Project) at the University of Sheffield.

Contributors

Helen Barber is a Montessori teacher, lecturer and tutor.

Karen Boardman is a nursery teacher in independent education, having spent seven years teaching early years' practitioners in further and higher education in Merseyside.

Di Chilvers has been a nursery nurse, nursery teacher and further education lecturer. She now works at Sheffield Hallam University.

Jan Christmas is a nursery/infant teacher in a small rural primary school.

Claire Cook is currently employed by North East Lincolnshire Council as a research officer in the Early Years and Childcare Department.

Heather Davies is a lecturer in Early Years Education and Science at a university in the north of England.

Elaine Dean is an advisory teacher for Oldham Early Years Partnership.

Rachael Leslie teaches a class of Year 1 girls in an independent school in Sheffield.

Jools Page is the Senior Under Threes training and quality officer for Kent.

Rosemary Physick is an Early Years consultant with Wiltshire LEA.

Louise Short has lived in the United Arab Emirates for 20 years. She works for the government of Dubai.

Chris Stevens supports private and voluntary settings in implementing the Foundation Stage Curriculum.

Ceri Tacey taught in Nottingham before moving overseas to teach.

Alison Wakeford is a child rights consultant working in South East Asia, where she has been living for the last ten years.

Karen Wilkinson is a Bookstart officer for Wakefield library service.

Introduction

Kath Hirst

E arly Childhood in the UK has seen great change, with many recent new policies. In response to these policies, practice has been constantly changing, creating a challenge for those in the field. The authors in this collection have responded to the challenge.

The first part of the book focuses on *Early Childhood Services and Settings*, addressing issues such as children's rights and changing times. Legislative changes in recent years have affected Early Childhood provision in all settings: mainstream, voluntary and the independent sector. The chapters in this first section reflect issues pertinent not only to the UK but worldwide. Alison Wakeford opens with a discussion about whether the rights of ethnic minority children are being addressed in developing countries. The next three chapters, by Elaine Dean, Rosemary Physick and Chris Stevens, reflect on recent legislative changes that have affected practice in the voluntary sector. In chapter 5 Helen Barber highlights the need for greater communication and understanding between Montessori teachers and reception teachers in mainstream settings.

Part two focuses on *Gender and Difference in Provision and Play*. Claire Cook investigates reasons for the low percentage of men in the workforce in early childhood education. In chapter 7, Ceri Tacey investigates the home and school gender discourses of four and five year-old children in a small British military community. While Rachael Leslie's chapter 8 examines gender 'through girls' eyes'.

The final chapter in part two addresses the issue of inclusion for a young child living in Dubai. In 'Imogen's story', Louise Short draws our attention to the difference between 'inclusion' and 'integration'.

The final part of the book examines the *Adults' Influences on Children's Learning*. Jools Page interviews three leading academics in the UK on issues related to the under threes. Karen Boardman and Karen Wilkinson consider the role of the adult in contributing to children's early literacy development. Boardman shows how she used children's drawings to further children's learning and enhance her own teaching (chapter 11) and Wilkinson illustrates how children have clear views on their choice of books.

Adults' views on the role of play in a rural primary school are the focus of Jan Christmas's chapter 13. She concludes that both adults and children should feel that it is 'OK to play' in the primary school. Heather Davies focuses on how practitioners can support children's thinking skills in the Foundation Stage. Di Chilvers (chapter 15) concludes the collection by highlighting the importance of observing children and other adults, as a way of becoming a reflective practitioner.

We should like to thank all the contributors for allowing us to include their work in this book.

Part 1
EARLY CHILDHOOD SERVICES
AND SETTING

1

Early Childhood Education in developing countries: are ethnic minority children required to compromise their rights?

Alison Wakeford

This chapter focuses on the extent to which the rights of ethnic minority children are being met by international donors (such as Save the Children) working in education in developing nations. Programming strategies have tended to focus on two opposing approaches, either to meet the needs of children, or more recently, to fulfil their *rights*. While the two opposing approaches are underpinned by different theories, numerous obstacles have contributed to a system in which both approaches follow a similar path of working towards meeting children's needs.

This chapter draws on seven interviews with officials working as International Donor (ID), Vietnamese Official (VO) and Vietnamese National (VN) to examine the extent to which talk of *rights* is incorporated into education programming, making particular reference to current work in the Socialist Republic of Vietnam. The chapter discusses early education as a need and as a *right* in the policy context of Socialist Republic of Vietnam and, through an analysis of the two approaches, shows a continuing reliance on mass systems of education. It considers human rights as a basis for education programming and speculates on the viability of such an approach in some political situations. The research process, ethical considerations and constraints of the research context are also discussed.

Education: a basic need or a human right?

Traditionally international donors and their government partners have based their programming efforts on meeting children's basic needs. Meeting these universally agreed needs provides the basis for donors programming strategy through the provision of professional and finan-cial support, with the ultimate aim of improving children's social and economic well-being.

The Socialist Republic of Vietnam

Vietnam's 'doi moi' reform process during the last twenty years has changed the nation's economic mechanisms through the adoption of an open door policy and the engagement in international economic integra-tion. This has generated strength for the nation's development in taking measures which support human development (National Center for Social Sciences and Humanities, 2001).

Ethnic minorities in Vietnam

President Ho Chi Minh included reference to ethnic minority people as being part of Vietnamese society in the first constitution of Vietnam in 1946. With a total population of 76 million, the 53 ethnic minority groups in Vietnam constitute 13.8 per cent of the population (General Statistical Office/Committee for the Protection and Care of Children, 1999 p2). These ethnic minority groups are generally poverty stricken because of their traditionally large families. In an attempt to overcome such poverty, Vietnam's ethnic policy is aimed at:

> ...Creating favourable conditions for ethnic minority people to over-come their backward and poverty situation, to gradually improve their material and spiritual life and to integrate into the mainstream of the country... (Socialist Republic of Vietnam, 1999 p58)

The education system of Vietnam

Education has always had high priority in Vietnamese national policy. The Law on the Universalisation of Primary Education (1991) states that primary education is compulsory for every Vietnamese child between the ages of six and ten years. Vietnam has a primary enrolment rate of 93 per cent with 89 per cent of children reaching grade five (Socialist Republic of Vietnam, 2000b).

The current education strategy aims to reach an enrolment rate of 98 per cent and a primary school completion rate of 85-95 per cent by the year

2010 (Vietnamese official interview). To achieve this increase cost-effective measures have been introduced, including teachers working double shifts, multi-grade teaching and the increase of the primary school day from four hours to seven or eight (Vietnamese official interview).

Government policy to improve educational opportunities for ethnic minorities

Since 1991 the government has been trying to extend primary education to the highland regions via a multi-grade teaching project and more recently the introduction of boarding schools for ethnic minority children from the rural areas. In 2000 around 60,000 children attended boarding schools (Socialist Republic of Vietnam, 2000a p20). Overall enrolment levels of ethnic minority children at the primary level have improved dramatically (82.2 per cent in 1998/99, National Centre for Social Sciences and Humanities, 2001 Table 2.5).

The policy in Vietnam is for all students to learn and use Vietnamese as the national language. Due to the high drop out rates in the early primary years among ethnic minority pupils, pre-schools have been set up for five year olds so that they can become conversant in Vietnamese before they start school. Once in school, minority students may learn their minority language as a subject from grade three.

These policies pave the way for the development of a good comprehensive bilingual education programme to improve the teaching of the Vietnamese language and better integrate ethnic minority people into mainstream Vietnamese society (Vietnamese national interview). The programmes outlined above have expanded educational opportunity for ethnic minority children, through universal primary education. While there is still much to be done, the partnership of international donors and the government of Vietnam is on course to achieve universal primary education and expand this to the whole education system.

Human rights as a basis for programming

A rights-based approach to programming builds on a commitment to the fulfilment of human rights with emphasis on the rights of the individual. Human rights of children are not just *goals* of development but an essential feature in the *practice* of development.

A rights-based approach to programming involves a strategic move towards addressing the immediate *root causes* of particular problems and away from meeting children's immediate needs and the accompanying symptoms. It aims to achieve this strategic move through five basic principles in the programming strategy: accountability, participation, attention to vulnerability, best interests of the child and focusing on an holistic approach (Thei, 2001 p112). These issues, taken from the UN Convention on the Rights of the Child, have been addressed to varying degrees over the last decade, but the combination of these principles into an holistic strategic process is key to this approach. The five principles are closely interlinked but the following discussion examines each one individually.

Accountability

The defining basis of the rights-based approach to programming are *duties* and *obligations*. Rights-holders are entitled to rights while duty-bearers are the actors collectively responsible for the realisation of human rights. The duty bearer is the connection between the rights holder and their right, without a duty bearer fulfilling their obligation, the right remains out of reach (Hammarberg and Belembaogo, 2000).

Within a rights-based strategy, primary emphasis is placed on government's role to fulfil obligations and duties to its citizens, including children. Non Governmental Organisations (NGOs) and the media have a role to play as watchdog, to hold governments accountable and encourage them to fulfil their commitments. Programmatically a donor's role is to ensure that a government fulfils its obligations and provides support to achieve this. In this way a rights-based approach transforms goodwill, charity and benevolence into justice through a system of obligation, duty and responsibility (Save the Children (UK), 2000 p1).

The counterpart of states' obligations is the right of all people to make claims on governments and institutions. Thus the introduction of duties and obligations is the key factor in the development of a system of accountability that is to be given greater prominence and transparency and is ultimately non-negotiable.

The best interests of the child

An overarching principle of the UN Convention on the Rights of the Child, the best interests of the child, is of primary importance in the rights-based programming strategy. Duties and obligations of government, communities and parents ensure that within any decision-making process, the best interests of the child are of paramount concern.

Attention to vulnerability

The concept of positive discrimination is considered necessary to ensure that the most disadvantaged children in society have their rights assured.

Governments have a duty to promote ethnic minority cultures through the teaching and development of minority languages and protection of religious beliefs and practices, thus ensuring fulfilment of the right to a quality education rather than the view that receiving a poor education is better than receiving none.

Child participation
Children are seen as full human beings, as rights-holders who can play an active part in the fulfilment of their rights. By placing and ultimately accepting children of all ages as competent holders of rights, we can challenge adult assumptions about children, their abilities and competences and their role in society.

Ethnic minority people have a right to participate in the education process – an important shift from dependency to empowerment. Fundamental rights ensure that ethnic minority children hold the right to be equal, as well as the right to be different (Black, 1996; Hodgson, 1998). Although problematic the fulfilment of these two sometimes conflicting rights can be achieved through the principle of participation, which allows individuals to determine the appropriate balance.

Developing an holistic approach to programming
Rights-based programming is different from what has often been seen as child rights work or individual child rights programmes. This has given the impression that work on children's rights is a specific sector of work which is optional in programming rather than integral to all aspects of it (Donor Interview). Some sectors developed an holistic framework during the 1990s that makes it relatively easy to incorporate a rights-based approach. This is true of early childhood education and disability, which already consider the whole child in the broader context of society.

The move towards a rights-based approach has required international donors to make a tactical change in the practical work they undertake, moving from practical grass roots projects towards advocacy.

A rights-based approach aims to provide the opportunity for a more effective, sustainable and rational development process through the introduction of enhanced accountability, the identification of specific duties and duty-bearers, a focus on the best interests of the child and children's active participation within the education process.

A critique of rights-based programming
The UN Convention on the Rights of the Child emphasises the rights of the individual child over the rights of the community. This is often used

as a basis for attacking the rights rhetoric, as it appears in direct contrast to the cultural and societal norms of societies which place high importance on families and communities. Critics of the concept of human rights argue that it is ethnocentric, being founded upon a western philosophy of society and politics (Ferguson, 1999; Armstrong and Barton, 1999).

Accountability

As the ethos of rights-based programming is focused on the duty of governments, political will is the anchor of all subsequent work. Without legal recourse, the fulfilment of duties and obligations becomes a matter of goodwill. While the right to education is willingly acknowledged by all the signatories to the UN Convention on the Rights of the Child, the accompanying obligations and duties these rights impose upon governments, societies, communities, families and individuals often tend to be ignored or diluted (Lansdown, 2001 p46). Additionally, Vietnamese culture places strong emphasis on children's obligations to their families, community and country. Vietnam's report to the *Committee on the Rights of the Child* (Socialist Republic of Vietnam, 1999) clearly demonstrated the continuing focus on rights as a collective responsibility of community and people rather than an obligation of the state. This view of duties and obligations is further demonstrated in the *Law on Child Protection, Care and Education* where the section on child rights is entitled 'basic rights and obligations of children ' (General Statistical Office/ Committee for the Protection and Care of Children, 1999 p36).

The counterpart of a government's obligation is the right of all individuals to make a claim for the fulfilment of their rights. However, this presupposes the existence of state mechanisms for protection and justice for individuals, as well as a society where individuals are free to organise themselves around issues of common concern. In Vietnam, it is impossible for an individual to make a claim against the government.

While NGOs do not exist in Vietnam, the mass organisations that do exist have been created to complement government activities and the media plays no monitoring role (Save the Children (Sweden), 2000 p21-2).

The best interests of the child

As childhood varies among different cultures, so working within the principle of the best interests of the child is not straightforward. As the principle of the best interests of the child is focused on an individual child, problems arise in practical situations involving the idea of multiple children. In this scenario various interests often have to be balanced against each other (Donor interview). This balancing act becomes apparent when considering the plight of exceptionally disadvantaged children. For example, the government of Vietnam, with donor support, has fulfilled its duty to provide primary education to ethnic minority children living in remote areas, but this is a clear violation of a child's right to an education that is relevant to their culture and language, as well as the child's right to live within their own family environment.

Participation

Participation is a major aspect of the human rights perspective, yet it seems that children have a right to participate in the education process only within the universally held views of childhood, families and the education processes that already exist. It is this preoccupation with a politically and developmentally universal idea of education that ensures that development practice plays only lip service to participation rights.

Attention to vulnerability

The concept of positive discrimination, widely acknowledged as necessary to ensure improvements for disadvantaged groups, is often contrary to beliefs in the relevance of community rights. This is apparent in the government of Vietnam's classification of programmes on the basis of geographical areas, not making a distinction between the Kinh majority and the ethnic minority households living within the mountainous minority areas (Van de Walle and Gunewardena, 2000).

As well as placing the obligations and duties of fulfilling rights on the backs of the state, following a rights-based approach requires donors to refocus their work on advocacy, an area typically associated with unmeasurable outcomes. Additionally, the unwillingness of the individual states to allow withdrawal of considerable support, and in some cases sole provision of programmes, will ensure that opposition will be met while working within this approach.

The overriding dilemma is the issue of whether a rights-based approach can be effectively employed in an international arena where rights are not always acknowledged or understood. The ethos of duties and obligations requires an understanding and commitment which is unrealistic in the present climate. Thus, differences between a theoretical approach and its practical use are always problematic. Paolo Basurto, the UNICEF ICDC Director broached this at an Innocenti workshop, suggesting that in the near future 'the dilemma of taking a critical position against a government will arise in the eventuality that rights are not being fulfilled' (Black, 1996 p10).

This chapter analyses the two programming approaches used by international donors and governments to provide early childhood and primary education for ethnic minority children. Their use of the language of human rights, based within opposing theoretical positions, led to uncertainty that they could not achieve their stated aims with this style of approach. It is apparent that while the needs-based approach claimed to follow the principle of *rights*, it was overtly dependent on the traditional idea of providing financial and professional support to meet needs. Such a needs-based approach continues within a system which provides quantifiable measures of performance. It is thus easy to demonstrate success or impact.

To summarise, a 'rights-based' approach to programming is a way of thinking that aims to achieve more for all children. However, its viability is questionable unless it is located in an idealised democratic country with an open government that shares the social, economic and cultural views of the international human rights conventions.

Universalism or relativism?
The two programming approaches rely heavily on universal systems of mass education. My interest for further research concerns the dichotomy that exists between the concepts of universalism and relativism, with specific reference to the factors of culture, childhood and quality and their corresponding impact on early childhood programmes.

Traditionally, childhood has been viewed as a time of innocence, a preparation for life as an adult. Movement from childhood to adulthood was reached by careful progression through a series of universal stages of development. However, in recent years an alternative view of childhood has emerged which questions the global concept of childhood, viewing children as rights holders, as active members of society, capable of expressing their own views and ideas. To understand childhood within this perspective requires understanding the cultural codes in the society and communities where the child is located.

This re-focus challenges the theory of the universal stages of development and suggests a more relativistic, contextual and cultural approach to child development as cultural factors cannot just be wiped away to reveal a universal child-development core (Woodhead, 1999). While sharing this view, Kiltgaard (1994) questions further

> If culture should be taken into account and people have studied culture scientifically for a century or more, why don't we have well-developed links between those who study culture and those who make and manage development policy? (in Stephens, 1998 p122)

This narrow focus that has traditionally been placed on the development of the education system, as well as the overall goal of achieving 'school effectiveness' has not allowed space for consideration of important linkage between society, culture and school.

A number of studies have found immense variations in conceptualisations of childhood, as well as childrearing practices and beliefs (Hurenkamp, 1998 p5), while other studies have also found that early childhood education programmes are still often based on western ideals of childhood (Dahlberg *et al,* 1998; Arnold *et al,* 2000). It is this failure to provide even a cursory consideration of the local concepts of childhood that ensures that these programmes cannot be sustainable.

This redefining of education and childhood has caused problems of terminology. The use of the terms 'appropriate education' and 'effective education' could be considered problematic due to their implicit implication of a shared understanding of a proposed outcome. However Black suggests a distinct difference:

> Appropriate education may conflict with effective education. Effective education allows you to succeed according to majority norms. Appropriate education may simply be a romanticised version of education, and then it will reinforce marginalisation. (Black, 1996 p27)

In the context of this chapter, the term 'appropriate education' involves an education process that attempts to move outside traditional narrow guidelines of a national education programme. In effect it is an educational process that encapsulates an awareness of cultural and societal factors. Further research and evidence is required before Black's warning can be either accepted or rejected.

The underlying focus of this chapter is concern about the extent to which the educational rights of ethnic minorities are being fulfilled. At present it seems that rights are not being fulfilled to an adequate standard due to the obstacles that international donors have encountered with *human rights* as the underlying principle of their programming strategy. For this reason, many donors have diverted (or not re-focused) their basic programming strategy away from the easier option of meeting *needs* If a donor organisation is promoting its work as encompassing the fulfilment of human rights for children, without undertaking work towards this goal, we could ask 'Who is in a position to hold the donors accountable for their duties and obligations to the people of the nations they are working within?'

Research issues
The research context
The location of the study in the Socialist Republic of Vietnam, brought specific research issues to the fore. Options for research into child rights in Vietnam is limited due to the political situation and the closed nature of 'rights' as a topic. The study therefore draws on a theoretical analysis of programming approaches and is supplemented by interviews with seven officials who were either international donors, Vietnamese officials or Vietnamese nationals.

Methodological issues
The study involved a process of ideology critique whereby 'ideologies can be treated as a set of beliefs... designed to protect the interests of the majority' (Cohen *et al*, 2000 p33). This is particularly pertinent when discussing educational provision for children from ethnic minorities as attempts at improving the situation are only made within the existing universal system of mass education. Attention to the pertinent issues of bias and ethics and the effect these may have on the research process was crucial, especially with regard to the interview process.

To give fair voice to both perspectives, I wanted to interview the same number of officials representing 'needs-based' and 'rights-based' viewpoints. I was also aware that interviewees' perceptions of me as the interviewer could create some bias. For example, as a white English woman I might be regarded as a relative insider by a European international donor, but a Vietnamese national could well consider me to be an outsider. I was conscious of the potential effect of various insider/outsider perspectives on the social dynamics between me and the interviewees. I was also aware of undertones associated with additional pressures of cultural and political norms. I knew that talking to Vietnamese government officials would be problematic, with their strict adherence to the partyline, and whilst international donors are equally able to tow a line, I assumed they would be willing to analysis their positions.

The personal nature of interviews brought up a variety of ethical issues, such as informed consent, confidentiality and the risk of any undue consequence (for them) as a result of their involvement in the study. Face-to-face interviews cannot offer anonymity but I did ensure confidentiality for those involved and agreed how and where I could use their comments. Such confidentiality means that findings reported here are attributed to one of the three types of interviewee: International Donor, Vietnamese Official and Vietnamese National. These descriptions allow an understanding of the reference but protect the individuals because they do not disclose who said what.

The cultural and political situation in Vietnam requires recognition of the important of cultural norms related to meeting officials and undertaking interviews; the undesirability of directness during any social interaction meant that the questions could not be contentious or cause concern or embarrassment to the interviewee.

The study draws on seven interviews: three with expatriate members of the international donor community; three with Vietnamese nationals working in related ministries or government-led organisations, and one with a Vietnamese national working within an international organisation. When planning the interviews I was aware that the interview responses might simply reflect the strict guidelines of the strategy of the organisation where the interviewee was employed. Though much information was shared in the interviews, it reflected precisely that which could be found in their published documentation. I was not able to gauge the attitudes of those interviewed (apart from two interviews with international donors I had met previously). It was apparent that for Vietnamese nationals, human rights and the position of ethnic minorities were both issues about which it was better to have no personal views. I did wonder later whether I should have asked more difficult questions to push things further and uncover attitudes. On reflection this might have caused offence.

The interviews produced limited additional information but were useful in reinforcing my view of the vast chasm in thinking between the two approaches to education programming, particularly the unthreatening nature of following a *needs-based* approach within a nation where human rights are not actively debated. For this reason it would be interesting to attempt a similar study in a different national context where such issues are more open. This would make it possible to focus on the voices of the ethnic minority people themselves rather than rely on third parties.

This chapter has presented a critique of needs-based and rights-based programming in the context of the Socialist Republic of Vietnam and has highlighted the relationships in education programming between *human rights* and *meeting needs*. There is a need for further research and international comparison of approaches and effectiveness.

References

Armstrong F and Barton L (1999) 'Introduction' in Armstrong F and Barton L (eds) *Disability, Human Rights and Education* Buckingham: Open University Press, pp1-7

Arnold C, Bartlett S, Hill J, Khatwada C and Sapkota P (2000) *Bringing Up Children In A Changing World: Who's Right? Whose Rights?* Nepal: Save the

Children (Norway), Save the Children (US) and Save the Children (UK) / UNICEF

Black M (1996) *Children and Families of Ethnic Minorities, Immigrants and Indigenous Populations* Italy: UNICEF/ICDC

Cohen L, Manion L and Morrison K (2000) *Research Methods in Education* (5th edition) London: RoutledgeFalmer

Dahlberg D, Moss P and Pence A (1998) *Beyond Quality in Early Childhood Education and Care: Postmodern Perspectives* London: Falmer Press

Ferguson C (1999) *Global Social Policy Principles: Human Rights and Social Justice* Oxford: DFID

General Statistical Office/Committee for the Protection and Care of Children (1999) *Indicators on the Rights of the Child in Vietnam* Hanoi: Statistical Publishing House

Hammarberg, T and Belembaogo, A (2000) Proactive Measures Against Discrimination in Save the Children (Sweden) and UNICEF (South Asia) *Children's Rights: Turning Principles into Practice* Sweden: Save the Children (Sweden) and UNICEF (South Asia), pp15-30

Hodgson, D (1998) *The Human Right to Education* Sydney: Ashgate

Hurenkamp, M (1998) Culture or Context: What Makes Approaches Appropriate' in Bernard Van Leer *Early Childhood Matters* 90, pp17-20

Kiltgaard, R (1994) Taking culture into account: from 'Let's to how?' in I. Seralgin and I. Taboroff *Culture and development in Africa*. Washington: World Bank

Lansdown G (2001) Progress in Implementing the Rights in the Convention: Factors Helping and Hindering the Process in Hart S, Price Cohen C, Farrell Erickson M F and Flekkoy M (eds) *Children's Rights in Education* London: Jessica Kingsley Publishers, pp37-59

National Centre for Social Sciences and Humanities (2001) *National Human Development Report 2001: Doi Moi and Human Development in Vietnam* ONLINE: http//www.undp.org.vn/vnnhdr [accessed 31st January 2002]

Save the Children (UK) (2000) *Children's Rights: What's All This About Rights?* ONLINE: http//www.scuk.org.uk/childrights/main.html [accessed 17th June 2001]

Save the Children (Sweden) (2000) *An Assessment of Child Rights Training in Vietnam* Hanoi: Save the Children (Sweden)

Socialist Republic of Vietnam (1999) *National Report of the Implementation of the Rights of the Child 1993-1998* Hanoi: Government of Vietnam

Socialist Republic of Vietnam (2000a) *Committee on the Elimination of Racial Discrimination: Reports Submitted by States Parties under Article 9* ONLINE: http//www.unhchcr.ch/tbs/doc.nsf/ [accessed 27th May 2002]

Socialist Republic of Vietnam (2000b) *The EFA 2000 Assessment: Country Reports* ONLINE: http//www2.unesco.org/wef/countryreports/vietnam/rapport_1.html [accessed 26th July 2001]

Stephens, D (1998) Culture, education and development in V. Johnson, E. Ivan-Smith, G. Gordan, P. Pridmore and P. Scott (eds) *Stepping forward: children and young people's participation in the development process* London: Intermediate Technology Publications Ltd

Thei, J (2001) *Child Rights Training Materials* Bangkok: Save the Children (UK)

Van de Walle, D and Gunewardena, D (2000) *Sources of Ethnic Inequality in Vietnam* Washington: World Bank

Woodhead, M (1999) *Is there a Place for Work in Child Development?* Sweden: Save the Children Sweden

2

Reform or rejection?
The impact of change on the role
of the pre-school leader

Elaine Dean

Overview

This chapter discusses the perceptions of five playgroup leaders on the impact of change on their role and whether playgroups are being subjected to reform or rejection. Playgroup leaders discussed their role, working conditions, training opportunities, qualifications and the process of inspection. Their discussion highlights the role of a pre-school leader, exemplifying the professionalism of five women dedicated to providing a quality service for children under the age of five. It raises issues of inconsistency between government expectations and the lack of status and low income associated with childcare work. It suggests a widening divide between qualified teachers in mainstream settings and those working in the voluntary sector who are expected to meet similar criteria in pre-school provision.

The history of playgroups

Playgroups date back to the 1950s when parent co-operatives were formed in private homes or halls to fill the gap created by inadequate nursery provision for three and four year olds. These groups were few and far between (Brophy *et al*, 1992)). In 1961 Belle Tutaev wrote to the *Guardian* offering help to anybody who wanted to start up a playgroup.

She received letters from all over the country and playgroups burgeoned and grew. The Pre-school Playgroup Association (PPA) was set up in 1962 to offer support and training to playgroup volunteers and to promote the needs of children under five through conferences, meetings and pamphlets. Plowden recognised the contribution of playgroups to the expansion of nursery education but saw them as a 'stop gap' (CACE, 1968 para 324). In 1972 the *Education White Paper* promised major expansion in nursery education (DES, 1972 para 17). This did not materialise, or many playgroups would have been faced with closure. Pressure groups were formed in recognition of the priority playgroups gave parents, unlike nursery schools and classes at that time. Playgroups were said to have developed community links and improved the lives of children through educating their parents about educative practices (David, 1990). By 1975 playgroups catered for almost a quarter of three and four year olds in England and Wales (Pugh, 1988). In the late eighties, playgroups were mostly catering for middle class families, despite claims by the PPA that many groups were found in working class areas. The Government emphasised its plans to expand education for under fives and playgroups were seen as 'a permanent part of the scene, not a cheap substitute for nursery education but a valid alternative in their own right' (PPA, 1989 p6). The PPA argued that playgroups had 'an equal role to play with other agencies, in national and local strategies for pre-school provision' (Statham *et al,* 1990 p4). Despite playgroups expanding across England and Wales, they were not viewed as 'equals' in the provision of nursery education, many continuing to operate in poor conditions with low incomes.

Consequently a system of services for under fives has been created in the UK which differs from most of Europe. In 1998 the Labour government published co-ordinated childcare services and improved their quality (DfEE, 1998) enabling many playgroup workers to access training and professional development. A playgroup encompasses a range of services such as: 'providers of sessional care for children under five which are not in maintained schools and all those services providing longer periods of care which define themselves as playgroups' (Brophy *et al*, 1992 p 2). Parents may or may not be involved. The study was based on this definition, the terms 'pre-school' and 'playgroup' are used interchangeably.

Reform or rejection? The impact of change

Playgroups operate in an economic, social and political context that is constantly changing. What are the implications of these changes? How have playgroups responded? The implementation of the *Children Act*

1989 (DoH, 1991) brought about many changes. It became the duty of local authorities to ensure that young children received adequate care and education. Playgroups were one of the services subject to this regulation through registration and annual inspection. Barnes and Rogers (1997) argued that while the *Children Act* recognised the need to support day care providers, it gave local authorities power rather than a duty to provide (Children Act, section 3.34). There was limited access to training and whilst many education departments implemented nursery and reception class policies, little attention was paid to playgroups. This meant they had to adapt quickly to survive (Statham *et al*, 1990 p101). Issues of recruitment, support and supervision of playgroup staff came to the fore as their workload increased the requirements of new policies (*ibid*).

The expansion of nursery education was intended to be via private and voluntary providers. However, playgroups across the country were badly affected by the voucher scheme (DfEE/SCAA, 1996a 1996b) as they were only entitled to receive half the value of each voucher due to their lower running costs. Parents opted to spend their vouchers on 'proper school' for four year olds, leaving many children under the age of three in playgroups. Changes in curriculum (DfEE/SCAA, 1996a) and inspection regimes (DfEE/SCAA, 1996b) left many playgroups struggling alone. The *Childcare Challenge* (DfEE, 1998) was introduced to improve accessibility to childcare services. Playgroups benefited from this initiative by gaining extra funding for training, and in many instances for additional resources. Childcare and development partnerships were set up around the country to offer support and provide training for playgroup workers.

The introduction of the nursery grant in 1999 raised the status of playgroups significantly with funds allowing workers the minimum wage and some playgroup leaders to become salaried.

A foundation stage curriculum and inspection

The *Curriculum Guidance for the Foundation Stage* (QCA, 2000a) was launched for all children aged from three until the end of their reception year. Training was implemented for early years practitioners across all sectors. Playgroup leaders are inspected to ensure planning and assessment are implemented. In comparison to teachers they have not had access to in-depth training and their income is considerably lower. So are early years educators valued across all sectors, or is the divide increasing? Although playgroup workers have been given the opportunity to develop their knowledge and understanding of issues relating to early years education, there has been no chance for them to enhance their salary.

A career as a pre-school leader
The working environment

Playgroups are usually parent-managed groups run within the voluntary sector. Accommodation varies but is most commonly in church halls or community centres, often shared with other users, with resources stored away after each session. A small number of playgroups own their own premises but most pay rent (Statham *et al,* 1990, Brophy *et al*, 1992).

Low incomes – limited training opportunities

When playgroups first started workers were usually volunteers operating in poor conditions because this, at least, allowed them to develop knowledge and skills in child development, with expenses paid. There are still volunteers working in this way today, although most playgroups now have paid workers. Throughout the 1990s morale remained low due to lack of public recognition (Statham *et al,* 1990). Training opportunities for playgroup workers were restricted due to lack of funds, and support from local education authorities was generally poor (Statham *et al,* 1990). Brophy *et al* (1992) argue that low levels of pay and conditions of employment experienced by playgroup workers is due to a predominance of women employees in part-time unskilled/semi-skilled work. The National Commission on Education (1993) placed emphasis on appropriate training, yet Curtis and Hevey (1996) revealed that the majority of day care and pre-school education services in the United Kingdom had unqualified staff. National Vocational Qualifications (NVQs) in childcare were launched in 1991, but many playgroups were excluded because they had no funding. Moss *et al* (1995) revealed that a third of playgroup workers had no relevant qualifications. Studies in the past (Whitebook *et al,* 1990; Clarke-Stewart, 1991) highlighted the importance of levels of pay, training and education of staff in determining the standard of service provided in nursery education. They concluded that policy makers should develop a better understanding of their workers.

A new training framework (QCA, 1999) will help lead early years practitioners towards a new professionalism. 'It is important for everyone working with young children to have some training' asserts the QCA/DfEE (2000b p12) and funding is available to cover training costs. However, two aspects of training adults can be problematic: time and confidence. Many adults have to plan courses around family and other commitments such as employment (Rogers, 1996). It is not uncommon for adults to attend training with negative expectations, usually based on past experiences of education (McGivney, 1993). Funding is only part of the solution in raising the standard of qualifications.

Findings

The role of playgroup leaders

The position of playgroup workers is underresearched. The PLA continues to argue that the quality of service provided in playgroups is ultimately dependent upon the knowledge, skills and professionalism of the adults who work in them. Working conditions, salary and training opportunities determine the standard of service that is offered to young children (Whitebook, Howes and Phillips, 1990). Five women who are playgroup leaders talk about their work, their anxieties and their motivation.

Pay and working conditions

All five leaders receive payment for their role; Bella is paid a salary (of £183 per week) as she is employed all year round. But all have worked on a voluntary basis without pay at some point in their career. Tina, Mikki, Elise and Sam have only been able to receive the national minimum wage since the introduction of the nursery grant for three year olds. Hours per week vary but all said they worked many unpaid hours.

Three of the playgroup leaders worked in conditions that were less than ideal. However, the women were still enthusiastic about their work and determined to provide a high quality service.

Two of the groups operated in self-contained buildings and considered themselves fortunate. The other three leaders operated in shared premises, not specifically designed for young children, like the majority of playgroups. Extra work is created because equipment has to be brought out and put away each day – something they all accepted with resignation:

> **Bella** I used to have work on the walls torn down but not any more because I know a lot of people. I can leave the big things out on the stage like the cooker and the bikes. It's at your own risk but since September I haven't had anything damaged.

> **Mikki** I work in a tenants' hall. Every day, everything out and everything in and that includes tables and chairs. We can leave four chairs up against the wall but other groups leave them all over and we get the blame. They have a key to our cupboard and they use our equipment and leave it broken. They never put anything back in the same place, so when I open the cupboard everything falls on top of me.

The women described their work with pride and pleasure. Each was committed to her group and determined to provide a first-class service for the children. With the expanding workload and the need to meet national standards, time management was an issue. They had to take work home or lose contact with the children during the session. They did not complain but they made several references to not being teachers. One believed the job of a playgroup leader had two dimensions: staff management and early education, and the administration and business accounts. Time is found to deal with payment of rent, bills, insurance, wages and keeping a budget, staff appraisal, planning, assessment, record keeping and teaching children. They said:

> **Elsie** My forty hours never included anything to do with the wages. Now I have to do all the books until they balance, get them to the auditors, get them all checked. I have to arrange all the meetings for the playgroup and the committee meetings. I deal with the charity com-mission – filling out all the forms. I do all the planning, most of which I have to do at home or it wouldn't get done and I'm the SENCO.

> **Bella** I have to sort out the training and encourage my staff to go on courses. I do my planning and records at home because it is the only way. It is a lot of pressure that is building up more and more. We are becoming like nursery teachers.

> **Sam** At the end of the day we are not teachers, we haven't got teacher qualifications. It is hard work but I've got this far and I wouldn't like to give it all up.

Reform or rejection?

The women agreed that there had been many positive changes within the playgroup movement: they had recognition and the quality of service and funding had improved. However, all expressed concern about the in-creasing formality of the playgroup curriculum which was undermining a play-based approach. All acknowledged that the foundation stage had improved learning experiences for older children to some extent, but they believed formality was slowly being forced upon them and that the needs of younger children were being overlooked. They said:

> **Mikki** The children should be allowed to come and socialise and just chose what they want to do.

> **Tina** It is difficult because you have to teach them these learning outcomes and some are just too young.

The five said that many playgroups would be unable to cope with cur-rent demands:

> **Sam** It depends on where you are. Some are going to get rejected and left behind. The groups that are more established get better treated.

> **Elsie** People will get disheartened and give up.

Conclusion

The playgroup movement continues to be run by women paid low wages. Many positive initiatives have resulted in improved quality of service, funding and training. However, the role of the playgroup leader is becoming increasingly complex and playgroup workers are left to struggle on with little training or support. While the status of playgroups remains relatively low in the eyes of the public, the amount of administration, curriculum planning and assessment keeps mounting. A career structure for all childcare workers will enhance the profile of childcare as a credible profession.

References

Barnes, S and Rogers, R (1997) Registration and Inspection in Abbott. L and Moylett, H. (eds) *Working with the under – 3s: training and professional development.* Buckingham: Open University Press

Brophy, J, Statham, J and Moss, P (1992) *Playgroups in Practice.* London: HMSO

Central Advisory Council for Education (1968) *Children and their Primary Schools* Vol.1. London: HMSO

Clarke-Stewart, A (1991) Day care in the USA in Moss, P, and Melhuish, E (eds) *Current Issues in Day Care for Young Children.* London: HMSO

Curtis, A and Hevey, D (1996) Training to work in the early years, in Pugh, G (ed) *Contemporary issues in the Early Years – Working collaboratively for Children* (2nd ed). London: Paul Chapman/National Children's Bureau

David, T (1990) *Under Five – Under Educated?* Buckingham: Open University Press

Department for Education and Employment (1998) *The Childcare Challenge.* London: DfEE

Department for Education and Employment/School Curriculum and Assessment Authority (1996a) *Nursery Education Desirable Outcomes for Children's Learning on Entering Compulsory Schooling.* London: DfEE/SCAA

Department for Education and Employment/School Curriculum and Assessment Authority (1996b) *Nursery Education Scheme: The Next Steps.* London: DfEE/ SCAA

Department of Education and Science (DES, 1972) *Education: A Framework for Expansion.* London: HMSO

Department of Health (DoH) (1991) *Children Act Guidance and Regulations. Vol.2: Family Support, Day care and Educational Provision for Young Children.* London: HMSO

McGivney, V. (1993) Participation and Non-Participation: A Review of the Literature. In Edwards, R, Sieminski, S, and Zeldin, D *Adult Learners Education and Learning.* Buckingham: Open University

Moss, P, Owen, C, Statham, J, Bull, J, and Cameron, C (1995) *Survey of Day Care Providers in England and Wales 1995.* London: Thomas Coram Research Unit

National Commission on Education (1993) *Learning to Succeed,* London: Heinemann

Pre-School Play Group Association (PPA) (1989) *Submission on the Quality of Educational Experiences for Under Fives to the Department of Education and Science Committee of Enquiry*

Pugh. G. (1988) *Services for the Under Fives: Developing a Coordinated Approach.* London: National Children's Bureau

Qualifications and Curriculum Authority (QCA, 1999) *A Draft Framework for Training and Qualifications in Early Years Education Childcare and Play Work Sector.* Suffolk: Qualifications and Curriculum Authority Publications

Qualifications and Curriculum Authority (QCA 2000a) *Curriculum Guidance for the Foundation Stage*. London: QCA/DfEE

Qualifications and Curriculum Authority (QCA 2000b) *A Training Support Framework for the Foundation Stage*. London, QCA/DfEE

Rogers, A (1996) (2nd ed) *Teaching Adults*. Buckingham: Open University Press

Statham, J, Lloyd, E, Moss, P, Melhuish, E, Owen, C (1990) *Playgroups in a Changing World*. London: HMSO

Whitebrook, M, Howes, C, and Phillips, D (1990) *Who Cares? Childcare Teachers and the Quality of Care in America*. Executive Summary of the National Childcare Staffing Study, Childcare Employees Project

3

Changes and challenges: Pre-school practitioners' responses to policy change and development

Rosemary Physick

This chapter explores the reactions and responses of four long-serving pre-school practitioners to legislative changes. It draws on evidence gathered during interviews and discusses the impact of increasing demands upon both working and personal lives.

Introduction

The motivation for this study arose from experiences in my own career, which have given me a keen interest in the pre-school, non-maintained sector of early education. In 1992, I worked in a non-maintained nursery that was self-supporting, relying on fees and fund raising events. Several years later I became an adviser with an Early Years Development and Childcare Partnership (EYDCP) which took me back to the non-maintained sector. There had been rapid and radical changes in the intervening years:

■ Government funding is now available.

■ A foundation stage of education for children between the ages of three and five has been created with curriculum guidance for practitioners. (QCA, 2000)

■   Teachers like myself are now employed to offer support, guidance and training to practitioners working with three and four year olds.

■   Pre-school leaders and half their staff must now be qualified and their provision is subject to regular rigorous Ofsted inspection.

These changes have had profound effects upon practitioners, particularly those who had been involved in childcare for many years. Some apparently welcomed the new opportunities arising from policy developments, others seemed de-motivated by increasing expectations, finding the changes bewildering or even threatening.

Research Design
My interviewees were chosen according to age, experience and place of work. These four practitioners, Anne, Cathy, Debbie and Emma each had at least ten years' experience and who worked in pre-schools offering sessional care in shared or rented premises. The interviews were held at venues of their choice, two in their homes and two in their work settings.

The interview questions concerned:

■   The implementation of *The Children Act* (DoH, 1989)

■   The introduction of the *Nursery Education Voucher Scheme* (DfEE, 1996)

■   The implementation of the *Desirable Outcomes for Children's Learning* (DfEE/SCAA, 1996)

■   The establishment of Early Years Development and Childcare Partnerships

■   The establishment of The Foundation Stage of education, the *Curriculum Guidance* (QCA, 2000) and *Early Learning Goals* (QCA, 1999)

■   Inspection of childcare provision by Ofsted

The questions were posed in terms of effect or personal response. The four practitioners speak for themselves here, providing a powerful testimony. First I will introduce them:

Anne has been involved with her local playgroup for eighteen years, initially as a committee member when her first child attended the group. She was a little nervous during the interview and very modest about her own abilities. She did, however, have clear opinions and was willing to express them. She completed the Pre-school Playgroups Association's foundation course several years ago, and since then has attended a few further training sessions.

Cathy's involvement with her local playgroup began around eleven years ago. Her youngest son found it hard to settle, she stayed with him regularly, and when a member of staff left she was asked to replace her as a paid member of staff. She had previously been a registered child-minder. She was confident and open during the interview, happy to share her views, which she felt might be unusual. Cathy completed the PPA's foundation course several years ago but has since been resistant to further training.

Debbie's youngest child had particular needs and she stayed with him at playgroup until he started school. She was obviously missed after this and was often asked to help. Eventually, when a new playleader was needed she was persuaded to apply and was appointed. Debbie was cautious at first, watching me intently as if seeking my responses to her views. Eventually she relaxed and seemed to really enjoy speaking about her job and ideas. Debbie has done a considerable amount of training, beginning with the PLA foundation course and going on to do a Diploma in Pre-school Practice, a six month course about SEN, and several sessional training events.

Emma began her career in pre-school work as a committee member of her children's group. She has been a supervisor since 1992 and has worked in two groups. Initially Emma was very nervous, reading from notes made on the interview schedule but soon relaxed and began to speak more freely. Emma was unusual in my sample because she has a teaching qualification. She trained in the seventies but never taught in a school. She takes her work very seriously and is concerned about its quality. She completed a Diploma in Pre-school Practice in the early nineties, finding it hard work but enjoyable.

Findings

Four distinct themes emerged from the interview data:

- self-esteem and job satisfaction
- training
- curriculum and practice
- the inspection process

Each of these themes was further subdivided as in figure 3.1 on page 24. This chapter focuses on findings related to curriculum and practice.

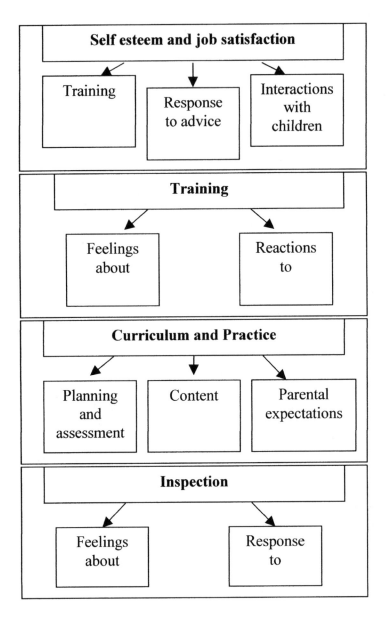

Figure 3:1 Subdivision of the four themes identified from practitioners interviews

Curriculum and Practice

How practitioners feel about their practice and the curriculum can be summarised thus:

■ They all find their jobs less enjoyable than in the past

■ The new requirements relating to paperwork, planning and assessment were felt to be excessive

■ The curriculum is seen by some as imposing too much structure

■ Some parents have come to expect more formal teaching, particularly in literacy

Debbie and Emma, who have higher levels of training, spoke largely about effects upon themselves of changes in their work. They have less time to interact with children because of the increased paperwork, but thought the curriculum was developmentally appropriate. Anne and Cathy were more concerned about the effects upon the children, interpreting the changes as requiring more direct teaching by practitioners. They questioned the requirement that planning and assessments should be recorded because it has led to greater formality. Play has always been the basis of provision for these practitioners, who appear to feel that the guidance and new expectations have led to radical changes in their practice.

Despite attending the training for the introduction of the curriculum guidance, Anne does not feel as qualified to cope with the demands of the curriculum,

> I suppose the actual curriculum side has knocked our confidence a lot really. Because you're not qualified you feel, oh gosh, we can't cope with all this, and you start thinking am I doing this right, should I be doing this, should I be doing that, and you start worrying, instead of just getting on and doing.

She has clear and simple ideas about the primary role of a pre-school as a place for children to develop their social skills, to mix and play with other children. She is concerned that the foundation stage curriculum is 'so involved', thinks 'some of it is too structured' and that it can alter the balance of relationships within groups, increasing the amount of time adults feel they should be working directly with the children,

> I think you have to be very careful that you don't start doing too much with them, because as soon as you sit down at an activity with them you change the relationship of the children with one another, because they're then interacting with you, rather than one another.

When asked about practice in the early days of her job she felt that little had changed, that there had always been a structure to the session and a variety of activities available during the morning. The greatest change she could identify between then and now was the paperwork, which she described as the 'main bugbear', 'there just seems to be so much... and it's just slowly increased'. Assessments were a particular concern: 'you're always wondering if you're doing the assessments correctly'.

Cathy's attitude to the curriculum and practice became clear through her views on the way changes have affected her job: she feels she is now expected to do more direct teaching and resists having to plan for particular aspects of children's learning. She demonstrated this by an example indicative of the frustration she evidently feels:

> You don't know what grey is? Right, this week we're going to do elephants! It's like, hang on a sec, every kid learns eventually at their own pace!

She seems to see the curriculum as an imposition that requires information to be force-fed, describing it as 'too serious'. She described her vision of the role of a playgroup as a place where children come to learn to be with each other, to get used to leaving their parents, to learn to share and where the session should be

> ...just a general, natural interaction, and gluing, painting and, yes you can put your hands in that sand, and it's OK that you've dropped some. Just natural things that take place in that morning, without it being too intensely... you know, 'What colour is that?' and 'Where is that?' and 'How many legs has that got?' I feel it's too much in their ears!

She said that the children's needs may be sidelined because of outside forces:

> I do feel sometimes that the education and the Ofsted and all that side of it (pause) it feels to me, far too (pause) more focused on than the actual kids. Who they are and what they need.

She also interpreted assessment as requiring practitioners to observe children in such a way as to remove their focus from the group as a whole:

> You're observing child A and child C, you know, you're writing it all down, meanwhile the kid behind you's hitting the other kid... you take your eyes off it while you're observing, so I do find it a bit too intense.

She likened the present situation in England to that in some developing countries, where children are taught to handle weapons at a very young age, and feels that too much pressure is being put on children – 'It's a great rat race already' and 'They're having their childhood taken away and I feel we shouldn't have to have that in this country'.

Debbie is concerned that pre-school education may be getting more didactic and subject-based; she listed academic subjects saying,

> All that comes later, there's lots of time for those, but if they're not emotionally developed, and if they're not socially developed, able to work with the other children, able to relate to adults,... they're going to have a heck of a job once they go into a reception class.

Debbie is clearly a thoughtful practitioner who reflects on her own practice, and has strong views about what children should experience. She thinks the six areas of learning are a 'good idea', and recognises the value of planning the sessions, but feels that the requirements for written planning are excessive. She said that she had always planned sessions but felt that one of the most important skills of her job was to be flexible and to be able to adapt to the mood of the group or to unexpected events. Debbie expressed concerns about assessments, questioning whether parents wanted written records to be kept on young children at pre-school; 'I think they bring them to a pre-school because they want them to play with other children, share...'.

She has found the increasing paperwork 'heavy going', and that when you remove the layers of red tape and the 'wordy bits' from all the recent advice,

> it comes down to basically what we're doing anyway, but you're having to write about it now. It just seems an awfully long-winded way round of telling people what to do when they've been doing it anyway.

One of Emma's main concerns about curricular changes was the effect, as she sees, on parental expectations. She described parents being upset when their child cannot read or write their name:

> A parent's expectation in sending a child to playgroup now is that they're actually going to sit down and physically write. And it's not! ...And you have to say, yes but, hang on, we are a *play*group, we are not a school. We are teaching your child through play. They've got to learn to socialise before they can begin to do all the bits you think they're coming here to do.

Emma said little about the curriculum guidance: 'I have read it and yes it's a help', and relies on planning and other curriculum support materials from the EYDCP to provide a basis for her weekly planning, describing these as making her life much easier. She rolled her eyes in exasperation about the *Desirable Learning Outcomes*, which she had just got her 'head round' when the *Early Learning Goals* arrived. She did feel that the goals are better and more 'geared to this age' and that the outcomes were 'a lot harder'. She felt the introduction of a curriculum initially had detrimental effects for everyone, 'the children were being put through an awful lot when it wasn't necessary. It's the same with us really, we're put through a lot'. She finds planning and assessment time-consuming and said it was largely because of the necessity of recording assessments that she has less time to play, 'because you're assessing children all the time, you haven't got the time to sit there and play'. She plans in her own time and though she would like to involve other staff more, she explained that it was difficult to arrange this:

> We find it hard to even have planning sessions, because we don't get paid for them, and people don't want to work when they're not being paid for it. I can understand that.

Many comments suggested feelings of disempowerment, and some practitioners talked about how their confidence had decreased. Increased funding and training opportunities have been of great benefit to many but at the same time those in the non-maintained sector have been given little opportunity to join any debate. Many never wished or expected to continue their formal education. They earn little more than the minimum wage and feel they have been forced, rather than encouraged and supported, to become more professional or give up a job they enjoy. They do not have the support of a professional body and are expected to attend training, unpaid and in their own time. In short, they do not have the same support as teachers in their professional development. There is a lack of confidence among many practitioners which has been exploited. They have had to cope with the demands of those whom they assume must know better and been poorly rewarded, both personally and financially.

Conclusion

The four practitioners showed commitment and dedication in rising to challenges, combined with feelings of dissatisfaction with change. They were willing to devote a great deal of their personal unpaid time to meet the increasing demands of continuing to provide a service for the young children.

It has been argued that the success of the playgroup movement has enabled successive governments to renege responsibility for properly funded pre-school provision; 'from a Treasury point of view, playgroups are exceptionally cost-effective' (Jackson, 1993 p98). Now that changes in society necessitate more flexible childcare and evidence of the benefits of high-quality early education increases, government has begun to act. Funding has increased massively, as have expectations, often presented as new opportunities for those employed in the sector. Universally available high-quality provision may come in the future, but past failure by successive governments to fund early education has exacted a human cost amongst those dealing with present demands. Many practitioners working in the non-maintained sector have been treated with less respect than they deserve. The result is that some of them feel they are no longer good enough to do a job they have enjoyed for many years. Little wonder that some practitioners feel saddened and demoralised: they have been doing their best for many years and new policy implementations lead them to feel that their efforts were not good enough. If as a society we recognise the value of high-quality early education, it must be paid for and those who provide it must be valued and given the respect they deserve.

In the quest to raise standards in early education the best features of previous provision must be maintained: the caring child-centred approach, the practitioners' joy in being with young children, the warm and respectful care from those intimately involved with the community they serve. This is an exciting time of change and development in early education provision. Many challenges and dilemmas arise for all involved. Government, academics, practitioners and parents must have the commitment and determination to continue to rise to new challenges together in order to ensure high-quality, enriching early educational experience for our children.

References
Department for Education and Employment (1996) *Nursery education: Nursery Education Voucher Scheme*. London: DfEE

Department for Education and Employment/School Curriculum and Assessment Authority (1996) *Nursery Education Desirable Outcomes for children's learning on entering compulsory education*. London: DfEE/SCAA

Department Of Health (DoH) (1989) *The Children Act*. London: HMSO

Jackson, S. (1993) 'Under Fives: Thirty Years of No Progress?' in Pugh, G. (ed) *Thirty Years of Change for Children*. London: National Children's Bureau pp.92-114.

Qualifications and Curriculum Authority (QCA) (2000) *Curriculum Guidance for the Foundation Stage*. London: QCA/DfEE

Qualifications and Curriculum Authority (QCA) (1999) *Early Learning Goals*. London: QCA/DfEE

4

The value of Early Years Development Officers' support for voluntary pre-school playgroups

Chris Stevens

Introduction

The success of the government's National Childcare and Early Education Strategies depends on the involvement of private, voluntary and independent pre-school settings. This study concentrates on one of these important sectors, voluntary pre-school playgroups and the impact of the support which a group of qualified early years teachers offers them.

Pre-school playgroups have a long history of providing care and education for young children and their parents. Since the 1960s the *Pre-school Playgroups Association*, now the *Pre-school Learning Alliance* (PLA), has supported the development of these originally parent-led groups. The association's name change gives a clue to some of the developments which have occurred in the sector. 'Playgroups' have changed to 'Pre-schools' with an emphasis on 'learning'. Many groups still call themselves playgroups, but in the government's childcare strategy they sit within 'education' and not care. In 2002 Pre-school Playgroups provided 353,100 places for three and four-year olds. Of three and four year olds in England 51.89 per cent attended a playgroup (National Early Years Network, 2002).

Without this 'meagrely resourced part-time service dependant on cheap female labour' (Moss and Penn, 1996), the government could not hope to achieve its target of universal provision of nursery education for all three and four-year olds whose parents want it. Until the recent introduction of the Ofsted *National Care Standards* (2001), there has not been a national requirement for playgroup leaders to be qualified. The professional development opportunities for staff in pre-school playgroups have also been very limited.

The Early Years Development and Childcare Partnerships (EYDCPs) have been given the responsibility of ensuring that children in their area receive quality education and care. Every nursery education provider is allowed the same amount of grant funding: the Department for Education and Employment Committee First Report (DfEE, 2000) noted that:

> It is unrealistic to expect the same quality from a well resourced nursery where there are graduate staff, to a setting where there are few resources or facilities and few qualified staff with possibly no qualified teachers. (DfEE, 2000 para 136)

However, this is the current expectation of Ofsted and the Department for Education and Skills (DfES).

The DfES has, by setting an achievement target for partnerships, introduced a system of qualified teacher support to voluntary, independent and private providers. These teams of qualified teachers must ensure that the Foundation Stage curriculum is implemented appropriately and that three and four year olds receive good quality education.

The county where I work has appointed a team of early years teachers, Early Years Development Officers (EYDOs) to support providers by carrying out individual visits to groups and by providing group training sessions. The service began in 1999 and by 2004 there were seven full time equivalent EYDOs providing support to approximately 300 groups. Visits to groups are prioritised according to identified needs.

EYDOs initially provided support around the early years curriculum but recent changes in legislation such as the National Care Standards (Ofsted, 2001) mean that support is needed in areas such as risk assessment and staff recruitment. This chapter reports an evaluation of the EYDO service. It aims to discover what impact the involvement of qualified teachers has had on the practice of voluntary pre-school playgroups in this county, and how this support has been received by the practitioners. Has it changed their practice?

The remit of EYDOs is to effect change and to improve the quality of pre-school playgroups. Practitioners, policy makers and many other stakeholders hold views about what constitutes quality and how it can be measured. EYDOs performance will be judged against Ofsted inspection results, but is this a fair way of assessing improvements?

Official reports, policy documents and much research have debated issues around 'quality' in the early years. The debate is also fuelled by the great variety of differing provision available to children and parents, such as local authority nurseries, playgroups, nursery schools and child-minders. It is clear from all this discussion that a clear definition of quality has not been reached.

However, the EYDOs must operate within the Ofsted Inspection system and the focus of their work must be to help pre-school groups to change their practice to achieve a good inspection report. The value given to inspection results by staff in the groups must also be acknowledged: it is the only official way their work with children is recognised. Groups are immensely proud and pleased to receive a good result. A poor result can mean great disappointment and the resignation of supervisor and staff often follows.

The involvement of a qualified teacher in a pre-school playgroup should, in theory, mean that these poorly resourced groups, with small budgets and few qualified staff, should be able to provide nursery education on a par with well-resourced, qualified staff in mainstream settings. Indeed many do, but there are critics of this theory. Baldwin and Lloyd (2000) report that from the introduction of the *Desirable Learning Outcomes*, teachers in nursery classes doubted whether a nursery education curri-culum could be delivered equally well in pre-school playgroups. Staff in playgroups may also lack the conviction that they can provide the same standard of education as nursery classes. Parents often choose nursery classes and schools in preference to pre-school groups, remarking that they want their children to 'learn' in school and not just 'play'.

For many pre-school playgroups, the introduction of curriculum guidance was a major change in practice and many still struggle with planning and assessment regimes. Changing from a 'care' to an 'educa-tion' setting is not an easy process.

EYDOs offer support to playgroups in two ways:

■ by providing Training Opportunities i.e. short courses and con-ferences

■ by individual support visits to settings.

In-service training and development opportunities
Pre-school playgroups had few support and professional development opportunities until the recent introduction of partnerships. The pre-school playgroup movement is rooted in a strong history of parental involvement, including parents leading the groups. Opportunities for

professional or personal development of the staff have been limited, compared with the opportunities for staff training in maintained nursery settings. Many playgroups operate on a shoe-string, barely making enough money to pay their staff. The introduction of the minimum wage and paid holiday entitlement had a huge effect on many groups. Few have sufficient finances to send staff on training, or pay for supply cover. Until the EYDCPs began to offer subsidised training, many staff had never had professional development opportunities, with training restricted to the areas needed to satisfy Social Services Registration, such as First Aid and Child Protection.

Support from Early Years Development Officers

Pascal *et al* (1994) found that the support of an advisory teacher, or mentor was a key element in the development of early years staff. They then had someone to act as a facilitator to the staff team, helping them to plan their professional development and review their effectiveness. This is the role of an EYDO.

This chapter focuses on the approachability, friendliness and helpfulness of the EYDOs who have early years skills and knowledge to carry out their role successfully but also have the right personality. Dean (1992) agrees that some advisory teachers have been better at offering advice than others; not necessarily the quality of the advice but how it was presented. Interpersonal skills are essential, especially when building a relationship with a group of staff. First impressions are important, so the induction programme for EYDOs includes training on making the first telephone call and the first visit and on comments made during the first few visits. Actively listening, encouraging and building up the confidence of groups demoralised from pressure of work is vital. Dean succinctly describes the strategy which the EYDO team adopts:

> ...the strategy is to make others believe that they are important, and their contribution is valued and that their point of view is understood. (Dean, 1992 p35).

An EYDO needs to understand the culture of the group and to use negotiating skills as well as possess the power to persuade practitioners that change is worth making.

Implementing change

EYDOs have brought about many changes in playgroups. The impact of their visits has been one of the major changes for playgroups. The Foundation Stage Curriculum, the most recent Code of Practice for SEN and the need for an identified SENCO and Ofsted inspections have all been implemented with the help of EYDOs sensitive to the anxiety, uncertainty and stress affecting people going through a period of change.

Aims and purpose of the study

The aim of this research was to discover whether the involvement of qualified teachers in voluntary pre-school playgroups positively impacted on the practice of the groups. It also aimed to show whether practitioners felt the service had been useful, whether EYDOs had been perceived in the settings as supportive, friendly and helpful, as planned, and whether the training provided had enthused them with new ideas and changed their practice.

Research design and methodology

One of the challenges of this research was to focus on the changes which have been made. Practice differs considerably from one setting to another. What is seen as good work in one setting by one person may be viewed in a different way by another. Improvement cannot be easily measured, whereas changes can be reported.

The task was to evaluate the effectiveness of support provided by the EYDOs from the perspective of practitioners and the qualified teachers.

The following questions were asked:

■ How friendly and approachable are Development Officers?

■ Do practitioners find the visits useful?

■ What other types of support would be useful to practitioners?

■ Have training courses been helpful?

■ Has the qualified teacher support changed the practice in the groups?

This chapter reports practitioners' opinions, obtained by a postal survey from 138 practitioners who chose to respond to a questionnaire sent to some 300 groups. A rating scale was used in the questionnaire where participants were asked to rate their answer on a five point scale or n/a (not applicable).

Research findings

The results of the survey were positive; changes had been made in the voluntary pre-school playgroups due to the involvement of the qualified teachers. The service EYDOs offered had been well received and the support considered valuable. There were only a few differences in the perceptions of EYDOs and practitioners and these may be due to differing expectations.

Main Role of the EYDO

Respondents were asked to state what they felt the main role of an EYDO to be. One EYDO succinctly described her role as to:

> Encourage the setting to plan a challenging, exciting curriculum that covers the ELGs (Early Learning Goals) and works to the principles of the guidance. Give settings the knowledge and confidence to plan interactive, play based, fun sessions for children and to assess what their next steps are.

Other comments from EYDOs were similar:

> (To) raise quality of learning by positive interventions built on trust.

The role was defined as encouraging, supportive, advisory, facilitative and as implementing the Foundation Stage Curriculum and improving quality. Overall the EYDO team saw their role as one of positive intervention and support.

Practitioners expressed a similar view. 'Help', 'support', 'guidance', 'advise', 'encourage' were the most frequently used words in their responses. Typical responses were:

> 'to help support and advise early years settings'
> 'to give advice and help wherever needed'
> 'to give reassurance and support'.

Practitioners clearly saw the role of the EYDO as supportive and not intrusive. Many statements relating to support and guidance were qualified by 'when needed' or 'where necessary', which implies that the support given was targeted at the individual needs of the practitioner or the setting. The practitioners were at ease with the EYDOs and used them as sources of information and help. This is reinforced by the number of settings (106 out of 138, 77%) who have contacted their EYDO for support and advice in between visits.

Although the EYDOs saw their support role as clearly relating to the Foundation Stage Curriculum and its implementation, groups saw them as able to offer support in many different areas. The demise of the Social Services Registration and Inspection Officers means that EYDOs are now being expected to support all areas of a playgroup's work.

EYDOs are also expected to keep groups up to date and well informed about new legislation and government guidelines. Practitioners commented:

> (They) help us comply with government rules and regulations.

> (They) introduce and help us be prepared for changes in childcare regulations.

The playgroup sector has never before been subject to so much centrally imposed legislation. It is hardly surprising that they are keen to access any available local support.

EYDOs act as advisors and mentors to practitioners. Dean (1992) points out that some advisors are better than others at offering acceptable advice. This is not always a matter of the quality of advice which is offered, but the way in which it is presented. One way to influence people is to act as a critical friend, become trusted, give encouragement and praise, and then gently suggest changes. In the development of the EYDO role this concept has been of paramount importance. Building relationships with groups has been one of their main objectives over the last two years. Respondents were asked to rate how friendly and approachable they felt their EYDO was. Out of 138 groups 129 (93%) felt that their EYDOs were very approachable.

Individual support visits

Respondents were asked to rate how useful EYDO support visits were in helping them to meet an identified list of priorities. The priorities were identified by the EYDO team as necessary to meet the requirements of Nursery Grant Funding and the Foundation Stage Curriculum and are the main focus of their work.

Groups felt that EYDO support was most useful in helping them to plan the curriculum, implement the Early Learning Goals, develop assessment records and prepare for Ofsted nursery inspections. EYDO responses were similar: they felt they had helped groups to implement changes in the same areas.

Practitioners thought that EYDO visits provided positive help in developing assessment records and techniques and rated the support highly. When EYDOs began working in playgroups many of them had no assessment and record-keeping procedures, a few had simple tick lists, and a minority had effective procedures in place. With the EYDO support, and as it is an Ofsted requirement, all groups will have implemented some level of record keeping. Many groups reported that they now had 'new assessment records', were 'planning children's assessments', had 'observation on all the children and each term we discuss children's progress'.

Groups have changed their practice and implemented new procedures partly due to the involvement of an EYDO. However, development officers have mixed views about the depth of knowledge which practitioners have in this area and of the quality of the records developed so far. The assessment training course was one of the least popular of the training courses provided (it was ranked tenth out of twelve in this survey). Only 72 out of 138 respondents cited attendance at this course by themselves or by a member of staff. This area is frequently discussed at EYDO team meetings as one which needs further development. The EYDO team is also guided by Ofsted nursery inspection findings. A recent report on the quality of nursery education (Ofsted, 2000b) stated that in almost half the settings attended by three year olds inspected:

> Staff do not assess children's attainment and progress effectively. For example staff do not record their observations of children's responses to activities, or, if such observations are recorded, they are not used to identify particular learning needs, and to help inform further planning. (Ofsted, 2000b para. 33 p10).

Analysis of the county's inspection results Ofsted (2001) also revealed that the 'quality of teaching', which includes assessment and record keeping, was low scoring in comparison to other curriculum areas.

Although the quality of teaching is higher than the national percentage (75.7%), in this county it is seen as a weak area, with only 'implementing action plans' scoring a lower percentage (59.5%). Assessment and record keeping will continue to be a priority for EYDOs.

Methods of support

Table 4.1 shows which type of support settings found most valuable in improving practice.

When asked why they thought that some types of support were more valuable than others, EYDOs suggested:

> 'I believe that continuous 1:1 support has a far greater impact on development than the 'short sharp shock' of a one off training course.'

> 'Individual support enables us to give 'tailored' information specific to the setting.'

Training was seen to be valuable by the EYDOs – though with reservations:

> '...but not guaranteed to improve practice. If the information is to be used and cascaded to the rest of the staff it needs further EYDO support to ensure this happens.'

> 'Settings sometimes leave the ideas in the room. They don't always have the power to implement the changes in the setting.'

There was an impression that people at different settings enjoy meeting and talking to other practitioners. However EYDOs commented:

> 'not all 'favourite' ideas are good ones'

Table 4.1: Practitioners' views of the type of support which was most valuable in improving practice

Type of support	1	2	3	4	5	Total of 4 and 5 responses
The opportunity to talk to people from other settings	2	1	11	41	80	121
The EYDO visiting my setting and offering individual support	3	3	9	33	81	114
Attending Training Courses	2	5	23	43	57	100
Going to a Conference	6	12	30	27	39	66

1 = Not very useful to 5 Very useful

'some find this very useful but (it) can depend on the characters and the quality of the pre-school!'

The opportunity to talk to practitioners in other settings and individual visits gave the most valuable support to practitioners compared with attending a training course. EYDOs agreed that individual visits and training, especially when concepts are reinforced on support visits, are valuable but there were mixed views about whether it was supportive for practitioners in different settings to talk to each other.

Playgroup staff can often feel isolated. In this survey they expressed their gratitude for an EYDO's support and the encouragement and re-assurance this gives them:

'[They're] always available to talk to with any problems. If they can't deal with it – they find out!'

'We would love to see our EYDO more often – even if it's just to stay in contact. Nursery life is always so busy, and there never seems to be time to talk, so more regular contact would help!'

'Very cheery and positive. Her attitude puts our minds at rest over anything we are worried about!'

'We like to have one person to contact regarding any problems. When not attached to a school we do feel a little 'lost' at times.'

'[She's good at] boosting our confidence. When the group is praised it gives you a great sense of pride in your work!'

Hevey and Curtis (1996) list the qualities which make a competent early years teacher. S/he should be: 'A well-adjusted person with a positive self-image' (p225). If by talking to an EYDO, or with other settings, practitioners feel encouraged, supported and confident, their self-image will become more positive which, in time, should impact on their motivation and commitment towards the playgroup and the children.

Anecdotal evidence from EYDOs suggests that many playgroups are demoralised by the government's expectations of them. They feel that they are competing with nursery schools and classes, but are certainly not treated comparably as regards resources and financial rewards. The DfEE Report *Tomorrow's Children* (1999) pointed out that many pre-schools are operating in circumstances which mean that they are unable to offer the highest quality of provision:

> They have struggled for years with few resources, resulting in low wages, little equipment and often inadequate premises. (DfEE, 1999 p57).

Some of the practitioners in this survey supported this view and ex-pressed the following concerns:

> As we are only a playgroup we feel that the expectations are too high compared with the nursery schools.

> People have low opinions of pre-school playgroups and we are not treated as important.

> EYDOs would not be necessary if the settings received sufficient finances to meet criteria. They could employ qualified staff with the necessary training and be equal to LEA settings. We need valuing please.

If the training opportunities and individual support visits provided by EYDOs boost morale in the playgroup sector, this will have a positive effect on practice. This study found that changes were already taking place.

Conclusion
Overall Changes
Appreciation of the support given by EYDOs was immense and prac-titioners were eager to detail the support they had received and the changes they had been able to make.

Respondents were asked 'Overall has the support offered, changed what you do in your setting?' Out of 138 responses, 91 replied Yes and 37 replied No. All EYDOs thought that their support had changed practice.

The responses by both groups on the types of changes which had taken place were very similar. The following three areas were identified by both groups as the major areas of change:

■ planning

■ record keeping and assessment

■ paperwork i.e. written policies and procedures.

The work of EYDOs has certainly made a big difference to playgroup practice and consequently to the quality of experience offered to children within the groups.

References
Baldwin, P, and Lloyd, S (2000) *The foundations of high standards – early years and childcare provision* London: The education network

Dean, J (1992) *Inspecting and Advising. A Handbook for Inspectors, Advisers and Advisory Teachers.* London: Routledge.

Department for Education and Employment (1999) *Tomorrow's Children: the review of pre-schools and playgroups and the Government's response.* London: Department for Education and Employment.

DfEE (2000) Education and Employment Committee, First Report *Early Years.* London: Education Sub-Committee.

Hevey, D and Curtis A (1996) Training to work in the Early Years, in Pugh G (ed) *Contemporary Issues in the Early Years. Working Collaboratively for Children.* London: Paul Chapman.

Moss, P, Penn, H (1996) *Transforming Nursery Education.* London: Paul Chapman.

National Early Years Network (2002) Lies, damn lies and statistics, in *Co-ordinate the Journal of the National Early Years Network,* 84, Spring 2002.

Ofsted (2000a) *The Quality of Nursery Education for Three and Four Year Olds.* 1999-2000. London: Ofsted.

Ofsted (2000b) *Profile of Nursery Education Inspections.* 1 April 1999 – 31 March 2000. LEA Derbyshire. London: Ofsted.

Ofsted (2001) *National Childcare Standards.* London: Ofsted.

Pascal, C, Bertram, T, Ramsden, F (1994) *The Effective Early Learning Research Project: The Quality Evaluation and Development Process.* Worcester: Worcester College of Higher Education.

5

Joining the 'Mainstream': transferring from a Montessori Nursery School to a state reception class

Helen Barber

No matter when or at what age children begin school, parents and teachers want children to be happy and to have a start that will help them settle quickly. (Fabian, 2002 p100)

'What happens when they leave you?'

What happens when they leave you?' 'How long can you go to a Montessori for then?' These are questions Montessori practitioners are asked, because there is a perception of discontinuity between experiencing a Montessori nursery setting and a non-Montessori primary school. As a Montessorian, the motivation for this study comes from being asked questions like these and having to rely on anecdotal answers.

Working in a 60-place private Montessori setting in a rural English county each July, all my key children left at age four (or almost four, if summer-born) to join their reception class. Achieving a smooth and successful transfer is naturally a professional concern. The majority of leavers joined the state system (in July 2002, 75%, in July 2001, 80%). Sunnybank, the Montessori setting in this study, receives nursery funding and works towards the *Early Learning Goals* of the *Foundation Stage*, believing they complement the Montessori environment.

To achieve a smooth transition, continuity and progression are required. For the children in this study, the Foundation Stage is split between two different settings whose differences are not only physical but philosophical. Whilst striving for continuity in the curriculum, continuity of methods must be considered (Curtis, 1986; Marshall, 1988). The *Early Learning Goals* are guidelines for a continuous curriculum but many areas of discontinuity remain (Fabian, 2002), which include transfer between different Early Years traditions. Dowling (1995) warns about focusing only on continuity in curriculum content, explaining the need to share information about a child's cognitive learning style.

A successful transfer depends on how well the pre-school and reception class communicate about how a child learns and how far their learning has progressed. Do differences in philosophy and pedagogy between Sunnybank and the four reception classes in this study result in discontinuities for the children which may impede their settling into school and the smooth progression of their learning?

Starting School

Critical impact of this early childhood experience is well documented. Yeboah (2002) provides a wide ranging international perspective. Fabian (1996), Dowling (1995), Marshall (1988) and Curtis (1986) discuss the impact anxiety and distress can have on a child's self-image and that teachers' expectations can have a causal effect on the children's transition between settings.

Children in this study start school at four years old in one intake. Anxious parents ask 'Will they be ready?' This idea of readiness and preparation carries dangers in itself (Nutbrown, 1999). Valuing a child's present achievement enhances self-esteem and emotional well-being, giving them confidence for the next stage, rather than trying to prepare them for it by pre-reading and pre-maths exercises (Clark, 1989; James and Prout, 1997; Fabian, 2002; Fisher, 2002).

David (1996 p99) writes of entitlement to good quality experiences now, 'that is, not 'pre' anything', but following an appropriate early years curriculum both as a 'current entitlement' and 'a foundation for later learning' (David, 1996 p96).

As a Montessori practitioner I found the most refreshing view to be that of Fabian looking back from school to pre-school and asking 'whether the school is prepared for the variety of settings that children will come from and be able to help children continue learning' (Fabian, 2002 p62). This is not shifting responsibility but putting the emphasis on something different, ie. our communication with the school and the parents' and the receiving schools' communication with us.

Literature on continuity, expectation and perception (Bennett and Kell, 1989; Kagan, 1991; Kernan and Hayes, 1999) indicates that well managed change can be stimulating. If discontinuities are foreseen, practitioners and parents can help children by teaching 'competences of resilience' (Fabian, 2000 p150), and develop strategies to help the children cope. The history of research into discontinuity is well rehearsed (Curtis, 1986; Marshall, 1988 and Clark, 1989). These studies of starting school base their discussion on what is still the only national data available, which is now over twenty years old. Many attitudinal and curriculum discontinuities have been helped by the introduction of the Foundation Stage, implemented in 2000, superseding some of these authors' concerns.

Discontinuities (scale of buildings and playgrounds, length of school day, having to cope with a different child-adult ratio, higher noise level and a more varied age range of children) still exist, as do those associated with timetables, change of routine, changes in style and content of language and social behaviour.

Fabian used the term *acculturation* to explain the child's need to learn about the culture of school in order to settle and enjoy social and emotional well-being (2002 p5). The importance of the parents' role in transfer to school, expectations of a child being informed by an individual's view of childhood and their view of how a child learns is well documented in early years literature and practice (David, 1996; Kernan and Hayes, 1999).

Research questions and methodology

Thinking in terms of the expectations and perceptions of the adults involved was key to forming research questions for this study. Kernan and Hayes (1999) were influential, stating

> ... the effects of a setting should be evaluated both in terms of the expressed values within the setting, and in terms of the expectations ascribed to it in associated settings such as the home. (Kernan and Hayes, 1999 p27)

The six Montessori practitioners at Sunnybank were approached for their views on the values within the setting. Reception teachers at the four main receiving primary schools, the local Early Years Adviser and parents were asked about their views and expectations of children who had attended a Montessori setting.

Issues that interested me were:

■ What were the Montessorians' expectations of the children's transfer to school?

■   What, if any, continuities or discontinuities did they expect the children to encounter?

■   What strengths or difficulties might the Montessori environment have provided which might affect the child in their reception class?

■   What were the reception teachers' expectations of children who had been attending a Montessori setting?

■   Did they have any perceived strengths or difficulties?

■   What were the local Early Years Advisers' observations of children making this transfer?

■   What was the parents' perception of how their child's nursery had prepared them for school?

■   How similar would all these views prove to be?

Ethical issues

This study was based in and around my workplace and the rural community where I live and work. There were several ethical issues to be considered, but one issue was peculiar to researching in Montessori settings. The particular nature of Montessori education in the UK in itself presents a difficulty. It is usually a private system, each Montessori setting run as a business. Asking for comments on the perceived strengths and/or difficulties of children from a particular setting may not be well received by the private owner – the question could be perceived as a threat to their business. The employer's agreement to the study was essential.

Interviewing the Montessorians, reception teachers and the early years adviser

Interviews were conducted with six Montessori practitioners, four reception teachers and the early years adviser. Reception teachers' interview questions were inspired by Bennett and Kell (1989) and focused on class grouping, structure of the day, their philosophy of education for four year olds and what was possible to achieve in their classroom. Questions on philosophy and procedures were inspired by Fabian (2002), as were questions to the Montessorians on pre-school preparation, the influence of the curriculum guidance for the Foundation Stage, and factors influencing children's settling into primary school. Interviewees were sent the interview schedule beforehand and interviews were recorded where practically possible.

Questionnaire to parents

Views of the reception children's parents on how well their child's pre-school had prepared them for school were gathered by means of a semi-structured questionnaire. Questions were about the details of the pre-school setting the child had attended; experiences which had helped them or caused difficulties when they started school; how well (in the parents' view) these pre-school experiences had prepared their children for school.

What did they say? What did I find out?

The adults involved enjoyed the opportunity to express their opinions, resulting in some interesting data.

All the Montessorians expected that *independence* would be the main strength children would derive from the Montessori setting, which would benefit them in their reception class. Social skills and skills for learning (*self-motivation, self-discipline, concentration and confidence*) were also highly valued. The focus of the reception teachers' expectations of children arriving from a Montessori setting centred around a perception of their being good at letters and numbers (only one of the Montessorians had mentioned this), and of the children being well-behaved. Two of the teachers expected good social skills from Montessori children. There was clearly some agreement and some mismatch of expectations in these responses. The role of any pre-school in a good transfer to school was not acknowledged by any of the teachers, unless they were prompted to discuss the transfer profile, which was not highly valued by the Montessori teachers.

Parents valued the socialising aspect of pre-schools (of all types) most highly, rating this almost equally with academic skills acquired at pre-school. This valuation and perception of the need for pre-reception academic achievement by the parents was not shared by either the Montessorians or the reception teachers. Perhaps parents and teachers need more information about each other's expectations? Closer convergence here would surely be better for the children.

All reception teachers were looking for competence in talking and listening skills on school entry. None of the Montessorians mentioned these, either as perceived strengths or as something they encouraged prior to school entry. Perhaps such skills are assumed to be included in Montessori definitions of *independence* and *confidence.*

One potential discontinuity identified by all six Montessorians was their belief that children would experience less individual attention from their reception teachers than they had enjoyed in their Montessori nursery setting. The rest of this chapter examines this anxiety in depth because, although it must be a natural concern about every child starting school, there are aspects related to Montessori philosophy and practice which require examination.

Individual attention for each child

The possible discontinuity of practice unanimously anticipated by all six Montessorians centres around the Montessori practice of practitioners working individually with children to introduce them to new activities. When the child is sufficiently familiar with the new activity she/he may choose to do it whenever they wish. From this foundation, children can choose their own activity and usually engage in it independently, rather than in a group. Montessorians call these brief introductions to an activity *presentations*. Such presentations are given in a graded sequence as the practitioner observes the individual child's readiness for them, or sees they have already learned these skills at home or in the nursery from other children.

Individual presentations and independent working

Why do Montessorians use individual presentations to introduce activities? Why do they think it is important?

> Following the norms established through experience, a teacher gradually presents now one object and now another to a child. (Montessori, 1988b p98)

> The lessons, then, are individual, and brevity must be one of their chief characteristics. (Montessori, 1964 p108)

Modelling precise movements in an individual presentation, the practitioner aims to encourage the development of co-ordination, fine and gross motor skills and independence as the child learns to be active and successful within the setting without adult help. The child is shown the complete cycle of activity from choosing the materials to clearing up after themselves when they have finished. Ability to complete this cycle aids development of concentration, encourages the growth of self-esteem and allows the children to choose their own activities and work independently with them.

> It is the perfect organisation of work, permitting the possibility of self-development and giving outlet for the energies, which procures for each child the beneficial and calming satisfaction. (Montessori, 1965 p187)

Maria Montessori foresaw the inevitable questions about these practices and wrote:

> Teachers... cannot understand how social behaviour is fostered in a Montessori school. They think it offers scholastic material, but not social material. They say, 'if the child does everything on his own, what becomes of social life?' (Montessori, 1988a p204)

The children operate as an active community, being inspired to learn from and help each other within a vertical classification rather than by age (Montessori, 1988a). Freedoms offered within the security of a Montessori setting include being able to be where you wish, with whom you wish and doing what you yourself have chosen to do. All activities are designed to be useful and developmentally appropriate, so that any choice is potentially a good one.

There is a place for grouping children either when they are new to the nursery environment, or according to children's spontaneous interest groups (Prochazka, 2000). Looking beyond this, older children (four year olds) form friendship groups and work within them, especially at activities they have initiated. The same applies to role play scenarios.

As a Montessori teacher I wondered about the effect on a child who moves from a Montessori environment, where most contact with adults has been on a one-to-one basis and they have been encouraged to be independent within a classroom, to a situation where they are asked to work in groups and where the adults interact mostly with groups of children, rather than individuals?

The Montessori teachers' views

I asked: What difficulties might children encounter when moving from a Montessori environment to a state reception class?

They responded:

> '...getting less one to one [attention] with the teacher' – Hannah.

> '...I think the only difficulty may be that they won't get as much individual attention as they get in a Montessori school and perhaps won't have quite as much freedom to choose what they'd like to do' – Carol.

> '...lower ratio of staff to children will mean less individual attention from teachers which the children may especially miss after being so used to the individual one to one teaching and attention they have had in the Montessori nursery' Jackie.

> '...Not so much individual attention and not so much freedom of choice' – Jane.

> '...Our ratio of children to teachers...they'll have nowhere near this in the school classroom, one-to-one attention will be far fewer times during the week' – Nora.

> '...we can implement them [the Early Learning Goals] in our system of one to one working but how will they work in a reception class of 30 children' – Connie.

Children's adjustment from spending some individual time with a practitioner to learning as part of a group was a concern of all the Montessori interviewees. Four of the interviewees were mothers whose own children had made this transfer, two of whom identified this as a difficulty their own children had experienced. This was the only potential difficulty foreseen by everyone and the only difficulty specifically related to a Montessori setting.

The reception teachers' views

The reception teachers were asked about the classroom routine including play and lunchtime, procedure for snacks, a typical day, proportion of time spent on teacher and child-directed activity, the nature of group work and the basis on which children were grouped. In each of the four schools the children are grouped and work within these groups. The teachers' comments on their use of individual work with children were:

> '...I teach individually within a group, the only thing I teach individually for is reading...that's the only time they're given specific individual attention' –Teacher A.

> Individual time with children is 'only for assessments and readers' – Teacher B.

> '...As there are only two reception age children in my class I do things in a group of two' –Teacher C.

> '...I hear individual readers. My classroom assistant works one to one with special needs children' –Teacher D.

For the children from Sunnybank, the reception class timetables showed much more structured use of time, moving between activities at an adult's bidding, working in groups decided by an adult and no individual work with an adult, apart from reading. This was a big change for the children presenting several discontinuities. Montessori and reception teachers have the same aims for the children in their care, such as developing social skills and a disposition to learn. However, the change between different ideologies is perfectly illustrated by the Montessori work cycle which is the time during a session when children are free to choose their own activities, which should be for at least two and a half to three hours (Isaacs, 2002), giving way to ability grouping for the second half of the Foundation Stage. Freedom of choice is replaced by increased organisation by the adults.

In Montessori settings, many children form spontaneous interest groups and friendship groups, listen to stories in groups and have Circle Time. But overall division of the class into groups and being part of an age-specific group is a new way of working for them and a new way for the children to see themselves.

How do children from a Montessori setting cope with working in groups? These were some reception teachers' views:

> 'No problems noticed, no, I didn't even realise you did individual work, so no' – Teacher A.

> I don't find it a problem [the children receiving less individual attention] but obviously that's something that's always going to happen – Teacher B.

Teacher C thought the Montessori children adapted well to group working. All children have to adapt to this to some extent. Obviously, focusing and staying on task is easier with an adult beside you, 'that's a natural part of being four, isn't it?'

> Some Montessori children do find it hard to adapt to group working. They are more likely to worry about things not being right if there is no adult guidance for their group activity...but some children don't find it difficult, it often seems to depend on the maturity of the child if they can cope with it or not. – Teacher D.

Teacher D raised reservations not raised by the others, that the children might be looking for and expecting more adult guidance and not appreciate the idea of being part of a group as easily as some of the others. This is demonstrated by talking when they are supposed to be focusing on a task. She makes the important point that all children are different and links the ability to adjust and cope to the child's maturity, which varies.

The reception teachers see that all children face the same problem when they start school because less individual attention will be paid to them by adults than they've been used to, whether in a pre-school setting or at home. It is part of growing up, part of the 'big school' package. Parents shared this view. So should the Montessorians be concerned over this?

Shared meanings, shared understandings
The opportunity to talk to the reception teachers was invaluable. Many positive and interesting areas of common ground were discovered. The importance for all practitioners of sharing an understanding of their work was clear to me all through the interviews with the teachers. Not completely understanding each other could mask discontinuities for some children. For the practitioners involved, this was important as they all contribute to the child's assessment in the Foundation Stage profile.

My main concern is that Montessori practitioners underestimate the amount of dialogue we need to have with reception teachers and that reception staff underestimate the importance of knowing about the philosophy and methods of the pre-schools they receive children from. Time and money are needed in order create opportunities to foster shared understandings.

Future questions and further research

This study provided the opportunity to begin exploring the perceptions and expectations of adults involved in children's transfer from a Montessori nursery to state reception classes. There was much to celebrate both in the children's achievements and in the increasing contact and conversations between early years practitioners from differing traditions. Joint training within the Foundation Stage and the EYDCP cluster group meetings have facilitated much of this, but it is always down to individual professionals to go one step further in trying to understand what their colleagues do to help children progress more easily into 'big school'. Research into reception teachers' and head teachers' understanding of the Montessori approach would further illustrate the need to continue dialogue.

The children have been subjects rather than active participants in this study: it would be illuminating to ask children who have moved from a Montessori setting to a state reception class how they see their experience.

The reception teachers interviewed were all looking for talking and listening skills at school entry. None of the Montessorians mentioned these skills as possible strengths or as something encouraged as preparation for school. Montessorians have a tradition of giving silent presentations for most practical life and sensorial materials, two areas of the Montessori curriculum. Perhaps this view of the importance of talking and listening skills influences their focus? It would be instructive to examine how these skills are developed and valued in Montessori nurseries.

Parents valued the pre-schools covering educational skills with their children more highly than the professionals did. There may be implications for staff training in effective communication with parents about this. Parents appear to need more information about the value of their child's experiences in pre-school. It would be interesting to examine how much parents know or wish to know about Montessori education and the reasons for sending their child to a Montessori nursery. The greater the match between the practitioners' and the parents' expectations, the better it would be for the child and the parents would be better equipped to support their child during transfer to school.

This study is a snapshot of the situation in one place, at one time. It is about the experience of ten practitioners, but it raises questions that may be relevant to others.

References

Bennett, N and Kell J. (1989) *A good start?* Oxford: Blackwell Education

Clark, M M (1989) Continuity, discontinuity and conflict in the education of under fives, *Education 3-13* June 1989, pp 44-48

Curtis, A (1986) *A curriculum for the pre-school child.* Windsor NFER-Nelson

David, T (1996) 'Curriculum in the early years' in Pugh G (ed) (2nd ed) *Contemporary issues in the early years.* London: Paul Chapman Publishing

Dowling, M (1995) *Starting school at 4: A joint endeavour.* London: Paul Chapman Publishing

Fabian, H (1996) Children starting school: parents in partnership, *Mentoring and Tutoring* 4(1) pp12-22

Fabian, H (2000) Small steps to starting school, *International Journal Of Early Years Education* 8(2) pp141-153

Fabian, H (2002) *Children starting school.* London: David Fulton Publishers

Fisher, J (2002) (2nd edn) *Starting from the child.* Buckingham: Open University Press

Isaacs, B (2002) The work cycle, *Montessori International* 11 (4) pp14-15

James, A and Prout, A (1997) Representing childhood : time and transition in the study of childhood in James, A and Prout, A (eds) (2nd edn) *Constructing and reconstructing childhood.* London: Falmer Press

Kagan, S L (1991) Moving from here to there in Spodek, B. and Saracho, O N (eds) *Issues in early childhood curriculum.* New York: Teachers College Press

Kernan, M and Hayes, N (1999) Parent and teacher expectations of four year olds in Ireland *Early Years,* 19 (2) pp26-37

Marshall, P (1988) *Transition and continuity in the educational process.* London: Kogan Page

Montessori, M (1964) *The Montessori method.* New York: Schocken Books

Montessori, M (1965) *Dr. Montessori's own handbook.* New York: Schocken Books

Montessori, M (1988a) *The absorbent mind.* Oxford: Clio Press

Montessori, M (1988b) *The discovery of the child.* Oxford: Clio Press

Nutbrown, C (1999) (2nd edn) *Threads of thinking.* London: Paul Chapman Publishing

Prochazka, H (2000) 'I'm not really a groupie' *Montessori International* 10 (1) pp27-28

Yeboah, D A (2002) Enhancing transition from early childhood phase to primary education: evidence from the research literature *Early Years* 22 (1) pp51-68

PART 2
GENDER AND DIFFERENCE IN PROVISION AND PLAY

6

'It's not what men do':
men in the early childhood workforce

Claire Cook

Introduction

Despite efforts to increase the numbers of men in the early years and childcare workforce, UK national figures show that approximately 2.8 per cent of nursery teachers, 2 per cent of day nursery staff, 1 per cent of pre-school playgroup staff and 1 per cent of childminders are men (DfES, 2002)

Advertising campaigns targeted at men clearly have little impact on increasing their representation within the Foundation Stage and pre-school childcare workforce. There have to be more deep-rooted reasons for the low numbers of men in the sector than that men have never considered it as a career option. Having more men working with under fives would surely have a positive impact on children, parents, the dynamics of the workforce and society at large. So why weren't more men coming forward?

Studies of men working with young children indicate that having a more balanced workforce would be beneficial for children, the workforce, parents and for society as a whole. The benefits for children include providing a balance of male and female perspectives (Lee, 1993), encouraging boys to believe that it is natural for men to care for children, (Nilsen and Manum, 1998), improving the academic achievements of boys (Gold and Reis, 1982) and providing a male role model of long-term presence, reliability and trust (Williams, 1998). The benefits to the workforce include promoting a healthy balance in the staff team, providing a challenge for female workers, providing an opportunity for colleagues to learn from different experiences (Men and Childcare Scotland, 2000) and providing opportunities for open debate and discussion (Jensen, 1996). Fathers would be encouraged to come into the nursery and become involved in the education of their child (Jensen, 1996; Ghedini *et al,* 1995). The benefits for society include promoting equality in the labour market (Jensen, 1996) and creating a more realistic representation of society for children in the nursery (Cameron, Moss and Owen, 1999).

Research suggests four main reasons for men not choosing to work with young children. These are career issues (such as pay, status and employment conditions), gender-biased attitudes (working with young children is an extension of mothering and is not masculine), fear of discrimination from family, colleges, employers, work colleagues and parents and the risk of false allegations of child abuse.

Most research into the issue of men working with young children has focused on the views of parents and early childhood workers. The study reported here investigates the views of tomorrow's workforce: current secondary school pupils in Year 10. Many young people aged fourteen and fifteen have fairly well developed ideas about what they would like to do once they leave school and if they had negative feelings about working with young children at this age, they would be unlikely to undertake childcare or foundation stage teacher training. The study examines young males' gender-biased attitudes towards careers, in particular careers involving young children, and their attitudes to work with young children and their reasons for these. It examines how young people, both male and female, felt about men working with young children and why they think there are so few men in the early childhood workforce.

Methods and methodology

The study was based on an eight question questionnaire where pupils were asked to state their gender, and how seriously they had considered their future career (they were given a list of 42 careers and asked to select which of these they would be interested in). These responses were later analysed to investigate whether pupils selected careers traditionally associated with their gender. Using the same list of 42 careers pupils were asked to state whether they felt each one was more suited to a man, a woman or either gender. These responses were analysed to see whether the pupils had gender-biased attitudes towards careers and if they did whether this was towards all careers or specific types of work, such as childcare. Pupils were asked whether and why they would like to work with children and which age groups they would prefer to work with. Given a list of 28 positive and negative statements relating to careers involving young children and/or men working with young children (relating to the four main reasons for the low numbers of men in early years), pupils were asked how strongly they agreed or disagreed with each. Finally, participants were asked if they wanted further information on careers involving young children and to receive the results of the study.

Three secondary schools in one local authority took part in the study and returned 212 fully completed questionnaires. This represented a 54.4 per cent response rate from the 390 questionnaires sent out. These schools covered the range of schools in North East Lincolnshire in terms of size and the areas served, including its rural nature and reflecting unemployment levels and other measures of disadvantage. The schools were asked to distribute the questionnaires to an equal number of boys and girls and to pupils of varying abilities and from the full range of ethnic groups. The pupils who took part in the survey came from a wide range of social and economic backgrounds.

Main findings
The study found that 38 per cent of the sample wanted a career involving children, 66 per cent of the female pupils and 12.5 per cent of the male pupils (a much higher percentage than the current proportion of men working with young children).

The most common reason was 'liking children' (5% of males and 40% of females), followed by a desire to want to help children to learn (1% of males and 11% of females). Four per cent of the female participants commented that working with children would be useful when they became parents themselves, saying: 'They are a good experience for you when you have a child of your own' and 'It would give me a head start for when I have a child'. Such comments support the view that early childhood careers are seen as an extension of mothering.

Boys were much more likely to express negative views about young children: 13 per cent felt children were annoying and 15 per cent felt working with children would be stressful. Female pupils were more likely to have specific concerns over controlling 'naughty' behaviour. One girl said she would not want to conform to stereotypes: 'It is so stereotyped that all women aged fifteen plus want to work with children, just because women are capable of having children.' Both girls and boys remarked that working with children might put them off having their own children. The most common reason cited by 20.5 per cent of male pupils for not wanting to work with children was that they wanted to do something els (9% of females said the same).

When the pupils were asked about their views about early childhood careers in terms of the type of work it involved: pay, status, and promotional opportunities, their views converged. Male and female pupils both had positive attitudes towards early childhood careers. The statements that caused the most negative views were those regarding:

■ promotional opportunities (they were more likely to believe that there were few opportunities)

■ whether teaching young children is easy (they were more likely to think that it was)

■ pay (they were more likely to believe that it was not well paid).

The biggest differences between the male and female pupils were about career opportunities, whether nurseries are important and whether teaching young children is about just keeping them safe and happy and not educating them, with the girls holding more positive views in each case. These findings support earlier research by Seifert (1984) who argued that men have more complex career aspirations, Penn and McQuail (1997), who found that women are more likely to be content with jobs with poor promotion opportunities and Moss and Penn (1996), who found that childcare is often perceived as an extension to the care provided by the family, rather than an education service. Although pay scored the most negatively, there was no significant difference between male and female pupils on this issue, which suggests that although all pupils recognise that early childhood careers are low paid, females are more willing to accept this (Penn and McQuail, 1997).

Gender-biased views

The respondents indicated that careers involving young children were more suited to women than men. Table 6.1 shows gender-biased views about suitability of careers for men and women. The small differences between the male and female pupils' scores were not statistically significant.

The pupils' views regarding gender-bias in early childhood careers showed that, although girls were somewhat less likely to express gender-biased views, and both boys and girls thought that careers involving young children were more suited to women than men, differences between attitudes were not statistically significant.

Niva (1996) found that women childcare workers doubt men's 'natural ability' to look after young children. This could be a potential source of discrimination against men in the early childhood workforce of the

Table 6.1: Gender Biased attitudes towards careers involving young children

Career	Gender-Bias	Males	Females
Nursery Teacher	Suited to a woman	69.6%	65%
	Suited to a man	0.9%	0%
	Suited to Either	29.5%	35%
	Don't Know	0%	0%
Infant School Teacher	Suited to a woman	55.4%	40%
	Suited to a man	0%	0%
	Suited to Either	44.6%	59%
	Don't Know	0%	1%
Child Support Assistant/Teacher's Aid/ Nursery Assistant	Suited to a woman	69.6%	57%
	Suited to a man	0%	1%
	Suited to Either	26.8%	39%
	Don't Know	3.6%	3%
Nanny/Nursery Nurse/Childminder	Suited to a woman	92%	84%
	Suited to a man	0.9%	0%
	Suited to Either	7.1%	16%
	Don't Know	0%	0%

future. However, a positive finding was that pupils did not see men who want to work with young children as being 'unnatural', which contradicts evidence provided by Yelland and Grieshaber (1998), that men who work in early childhood settings are not considered normal. This finding was very encouraging as it suggests that although a significantly lower number of men are choosing to work in the early childhood sector than women, men who do choose to work in the sector are not considered abnormal.

Fear of discrimination

The differences between the male and female pupils in terms of whether they thought that men working in the early childhood sector would face discrimination were not statistically significant. Fear of discrimination was not found to be a major barrier for men entering early childhood careers: the responses to the discrimination statements on the questionnaire were fairly positive.

Boys suggested that children's parents would be the biggest source of discrimination for male childcare workers (Wallace, 2001), whereas girls seemed to believe that female colleagues would be the biggest source of discrimination. The study did not find any evidence to suggest that males who want to work with young children would fear discrimination from their own family and friends (contradicting Cameron, Moss and Owen, 1999). This reinforces the idea that attitudes are changing and that society is becoming more accepting of men in such roles

Fear of allegations of child abuse

No significant differences were found between boys and girls on the statements regarding child protection issues around the topic of men working with young children though slightly more boys than girls indicated that men might feel uncomfortable when children needed a cuddle or to go to the toilet.

The most pertinent reason

Finally, the study investigated whether there were any significant correlations or differences between the four reasons for the low number of men in the early childhood workforce. The average scores for each of the reasons can be seen in Table 6.2.

Significant positive correlations were found between each of the reasons, which meant that the pupils who had a positive attitude regarding one were more likely to have a positive attitude to the others. This was no surprise, as there is a great overlap between the reasons. Out of the four reasons, stereotyped gender attitudes, were found to be the most prominent. There was no significant difference between gender attitudes and discrimination, which implies that fear of discrimination is equally prominent. Pupils, however, did not score highly on any of the four reasons. This suggests that there are either other factors to explain the low number of men in the workforce or that the way the data was obtained was not sensitive enough to reflect young people's attitudes accurately. Any research undertaken on this topic in future would really need a mixture of quantitative and qualitative methods, so that specific issues can be explored in more detail, and the complexity of the issue fully uncovered.

Table 6.2: Average scores for the reasons identified in the literature for the low number of men in the early childhood workforce

Average Career Issue Score (Mean)	Average Gender Attitude Score (Mean)	Average Discrimination Score (Mean)	Average Child Protection Score (Mean)
3.47	4.24	4.10	3.39

References

Cameron, C, Moss, P and Owen, C (1999) *Men in the nursery: gender and caring work.* London: Paul Chapman/Sage

Department for Education and Skills (2002) *Childcare workforce surveys 2001: overview.* London: DfES

Ghedini, P., Chandler, T., Whalley, M. and Moss, P. (1995) *Fathers, nurseries and childcare.* European Commission Equal Opportunities Unit/EC Childcare Network

Gold, D and Reis, M (1982) Male teacher effects on young children: A theoretical and empirical consideration, *Sex Roles*, 8(5), pp493-513

Jensen, J J (1996) Men as workers in childcare services: A discussion paper. *European commission network on childcare and other measures to reconcile employment and family responsibilities for women and men.* Brussels: European Equal Opportunities Unit

Lee, A (1993) Gender and geography, literacy, pedagogy and curriculum. Unpublished PhD thesis. Western Australia: Murdoch University

Men and Childcare Scotland (2000) Working Paper, January (ONLINE – http://www.international.mibnett.no/country/scotland/men_and_childcare_scotland.ht m)

Moss, P and Penn, H (1996). *Transforming nursery education.* London: Paul Chapman Publishing

Nilsen, T and Manum, L (1998) Masculine care: the nursery school as a man's workplace. In Owen *et al.* (eds) *Men as workers in services for young children: Issues of a mixed gender workforce.* Bedford Way Papers, Institute of Education: University of London.

Niva, L (1996) *Professional male child caregivers: A pilot study in the Adelaide metropolitan area.* Unpublished paper for the Graduate Diploma in Social Science (Child Development), The Institute of Early Childhood and Family Studies, University of South Australia, Magill, Adelaide

Penn, H and McQuail, S (1997) Childcare as a gendered occupation, *Department for Education and Employment Research Briefs, Research Report No 23*

Seifert, K (1984) Some problems of men in child care centre work. In S Pleck and J Sawyer (Eds.) *Men and masculinity.* New Jersey: Prentice Hall

Wallace, W (2001) Men Wanted, *Nursery World*, 24 May.

Williams, F (1998) Troubled masculinities in social policy discourses: Fatherhood. In J Popay, J Hearn and J Edwards (eds) *Men, gender divisions and welfare.* London: Routledge

Yelland, N and Grieshaber, S (1998) Blurring the edges, In N Yelland (ed) *Gender in early childhood.* London: Routledge

7

Why do boys like to build and girls like to draw? Gender issues in a small British military community

Ceri Tacey

Introduction

This study is set in an overseas British military community and reflects influences that are unique to this society. It explores the question, 'Why do the boys like to build and the girls like to draw?' I had become concerned by the apparent gender divide in the children's choice of activities in my foundation stage setting, and the potential impact this could be having on their overall development. Living in a military community, I was increasingly struck by the imbalance of power between men and women and the 'culturally specific categories through which we give meaning to our lives, practice our lives, invest emotionally in our lives and constitute our social structures' (MacNaughton, 1998 p158).

Discourses

The dominant discourses of society are the common theme of all the influences on children's gender development reported in this chapter. Through parents, family, friends, schools and the wider community they influence the way in which children see their gender roles (Davies, 1994; Gavey, 1997; MacNaughton, 1998; Thorne, 1993).

MacNaughton (1998) describes the categories specific to gender dis-course as those which represent gender roles, such as mother, daughter, father and son. The practices related to these roles are manifested through behaviour, clothing, thinking and feeling. The emotional invest-ments made in these roles are the ways in which we desire to perform them according to the dominant discourse of the society in which we live. Discourses are changeable from one community to another and within any given time (Gavey, 1997).

I aimed to open up the influences on these children's development of gender identity in terms of the dominant gender discourses surrounding them at home and at school. As Francis states:

> ...continuing analysis of the various gender discourses is required, in order to provide greater understanding of the ways in which we use them, their impacts on our lives, and potentially how we might resist or reconfigure them. (Francis, 2001 p75-76)

In analysing the discourses I hoped to develop effective ways of em-powering the children in 'resisting' them. I had not expected to find that I myself was one of the influences promoting the discourses I had hoped to help them to resist!

Methodology

At first I approached the project from a feminist viewpoint, concerned by the imbalance of power I observed between the genders in the class-room and in the military community at large. Further reading around the feminist viewpoint brought me to the conclusion that I was neither a liberal nor a radical feminist (Davies, 1994). I disagree with the liberal feminist stance that girls should have the right of access to male ways of being, because that reinforced the belief that the 'male' way is better (Smith, 1994). I also disagree with the radical feminist campaign to allow girls to be girls and not feel inferior for it, because this did not cater for the needs of boys or girls who wanted alternative ways of being (Davies, 1994). I believed that there are many different ways of being and to label them as being 'male' or 'female' was too restrictive (Lowe, 1998). Through post-structuralist theories, I was able to examine the ways in which the children developed their individual gender identities.

I used a qualitative, ethnographic approach which may be regarded as in keeping with the feminist stance (Maynard, 1994), as MacNaughton (1998) explains:

> Subjectivity' describes who we are and how we understand ourselves, consciously and unconsciously. These understandings are formed as we participate in, articulate and circulate discourse. (MacNaughton, 1998 p161)

By analysing the discourses of a particular society, post-structuralists are able to gain an understanding of a participant's subjectivity and how they come to their own particular ways of being. Ethnographers are also concerned with understanding the subjective world of their participants: 'In fact, ethnographic study is by its very nature interpretive, that is, it is concerned to understand the subjective world of human experience' (Siraj-Blatchford and Siraj-Blatchford, 2001 p194).

The open minded approach of both post-structuralism and ethnographic research makes the two approaches compatible. Ethnography is concerned with gaining insights into people's behaviour and actions, by making their implicit behaviours explicit.

> They are interested in generic patterns of behaviour because these represent the outward manifestation of internalised rules or codes of appropriate behaviours that comprise an individual's implicit knowledge how to behave appropriately as a member of a particular group or community. (Aubrey *et al,* 2000 p111-112)

The phrase 'internalised rules or codes' is in line with the post-structuralist analysis of discourses, where discourses are 'the internalised codes of appropriate behaviours of a community' (Aubrey *et al,* 2000). By taking a qualitative, ethnographic approach, I was able to examine the ways in which the children were influenced by 'internalised codes of behaviour' or discourses specific to their community, both at home and school. The qualitative approach allowed me to keep an open mind in my fieldwork, and be responsive to the data being collected and the behaviour of the subjects in the study. It also enabled me to take a fresh look at events that had become familiar to me and needed to be examined from an alternative point of view (Edwards, 2001).

Methods
Observation
Throughout the study I took on the role of participant observer. As class teacher, I was able to observe the children's daily interactions and talk to them openly about the study. During daily child-directed time I made semi-structured and unstructured observations of their play, which I used both to inform my teaching and as data for the research. Being a practitioner-observer (Edwards, 2001) had the added advantage of not needing a settling-in time where participants become accustomed to the presence of the researcher (Bogdan and Biklen,1998). The children and parents were already very familiar with me as their class teacher and were used to me observing their play and discussing gender issues with them. As an inside observer, I felt that the possibility of my presence as researcher

'distorting the system being examined' was greatly reduced (Edwards, 2001).

Videotaping

Videotaping was used to record long sequences of child-directed work. The taping was unstructured in that the photographer was given no particular themes or behaviours to look for, only to record long sequences of children at work, even if they felt the action was uninteresting. The main aim of the video recording was to provide some data form that could be re-visited after I had left the context of the study (Silverman, 2000). Inevitably some problems arose with the videotaping method. The restricted vision of the camera meant that there were occasions when the action went out of camera shot and the non-verbal cues could not be seen.

Many researchers feel that the presence of a video camera affects participants' behaviour in diverse ways (Aubrey *et al,* 2000; Rolfe, 2001). In my experience, the camera was not intrusive and did not affect the children's behaviour beyond the first five minutes. 'People can become accustomed and indifferent to anything in their environment, and a photographer is no exception' (Bogdan and Biklen, 1998 p102).

Fieldnotes

In the category of fieldnotes, I included notes taken of anecdotes from parents, observations of the children outside the classroom, statements made by participants and notes on my own process of reflexivity during the research process.

As Silverman comments: 'Obviously, in making fieldnotes, one is not simply recording data, but also analysing them' (Silverman, 2000 p126). As I made notes, I was very aware of making an initial analysis of the data and recorded how I felt about a particular incident or anecdote. In this way, the fieldnotes also became a record of personal reflexivity in relation to the data (Grieshaber, 2001; Silverman, 2000).

Parent Questionnaires

Parents were given a questionnaire, which used many open questions about how they felt their child's gender development had been influenced and several blank sheets of paper which invited parents to share any information they wished to.

Main findings

At the onset of this study, I agreed with Minns' (1985) view that my role in influencing the gender identity development of my class was in 'challenging the categories and perceptions the children meet outside' (Minns, 1985 p28). Elizabeth, Jane and Niall's mothers all discussed their commitment to gender equity openly. Jane's mother commented, 'I have always avoided the stereotyping of toys and outfits, and so Jane has generally followed her brother.' It was through interactions with these women that I realised that many parents felt that the stereotyped behaviour was influenced by school, not home as I had thought. This made me examine the influences of school and of myself more closely and was an important turning point in the study.

In response to the question 'Do you feel your child's behaviour or ideas about roles of boys and girls have changed in any way since starting school?' Daniel's mother wrote, 'Absolutely, he made no distinction before school.' She went on to give examples of comments made by Daniel at home since starting school, 'She's just a girl, 'Who wants to play chasing the girls?' and 'Buy her a Barbie for her birthday Mummy, that's what girls have.' For children like Daniel, who have no sisters or girls in the family, starting school may be their first daily interaction with girls. It is possible to trace two of Daniel's comments directly to school influences. The chasing of girls was a regular playground game, played by the majority of key stage one children and accompanied by the very chant that Daniel had repeated at home. Games such as this, where the genders compete against one another, effectively reinforce the gender divide. As Thorne argues, 'Cross-gender chasing dramatically affirms boundaries between boys and girls' (Thorne, 1993 p68).

Daniel's comment that girls have Barbies could also be attributed to school. All the children attended a weekly birthday assembly, which always included a discussion of the child's favourite presents. This assembly may be the source of comments from both Daniel and Joseph that 'Barbies are for girls.' Until he started school, Joseph had played with a Barbie at home, a change his mother attributed to school. Messner observed that: 'No amount of parental intervention could counter this devastating peer-induced injunction against boys' playing with Barbie' (Messner, 2000 p777). It is possible that Joseph was subject to a similar kind of peer pressure, when he realised that girls at school play with Barbies and boys do not, resulting in his comment to his mother: 'Barbies are yukky girlie' and his subsequently discarding the toy.

The school environment was influential in introducing children to other children on a daily basis and this had an impact on their development of gender identity and on raising some children's awareness of gender differences (labelling children, use of phrases such as 'good girl' and 'good boy', labelling of bathrooms as gender specific). By referring to children constantly in terms of their gender we were giving them the message that this aspect of their self-concept is the most important to us, and should therefore be the most important to them.

A picture soon emerged of parallel influences on children's development of gender identity, from both home and school. Far from being the source of challenging outside influences on children's perceptions of gender roles, school was actually a contributor. This came in many forms. At home, children were exposed to gender-specific clothing, toys and stereotypical role models of fathers who worked and mothers who cared for them. At school, they were exposed to gender-differentiated school uniforms, resources that subconsciously reinforced the dominant gender stereotypes and role models of female teachers and male maintenance staff. As Nichols comments: 'We need to recognise that both homes and classrooms are part of a discursive web in which discourses of child-hood, gender and learning continuously circulate' (Nichols, 2002 p142).

Home and school environments were influenced to some extent by the dominant discourses of society. Initially, this surprised me, and made me recognise that my actions were also affected by the dominant discourses I had intended to counteract. The most important finding of this research came from the observation of those families who were aware of the dominant discourses of society and were actively campaigning to counteract their influence on the gender identity development of their child. They consciously offered counter-arguments to the gender assumptions being offered by the discourses and refused to participate in traditional practises of gender-specific clothing and toys. In doing so, they effectively promoted the individuality of their children.

Elizabeth's mother talked openly about counteracting the views of gender, which Elizabeth 'brings home from school.' She used counter-arguments against the statements, 'girls don't wear blue' and 'only boys are soldiers because that's what Daddy does', to which her mother replied, 'I was a soldier'. She wrote about her concerns that since Eliza-beth started school she had started to comment on things that 'girls can't do'. She reflected, 'although it does not seem a big issue with her, I am particularly keen not to close any doors because of gender'.

Similar evidence of discourse awareness appeared in data collected from Jane's family. Jane received few gifts at birth as a result of the tragic death of her twin sister. Her mother commented, 'people were unsure whether to commiserate or congratulate me. She did receive a few pink things, although knowing my aversion to pink, few people tried this!'

Jane's mother did not adhere to the discourse that 'girls must wear pink' and consequently, Jane was not exposed to the first stage of gender identity development (Branthwaite, 1985). When asked if she felt that her siblings had influenced Jane's behaviour, her mother commented:

> Jane prefers her brother's toys to anything 'girlie.' She will climb anything he will, and generally would like to wear trousers to facilitate this. She just wants to keep up with him. She prefers Batman and Max Steele to Barbie, but enjoys the dressing up of these male dolls. Fancy dress is a big enjoyment of both children, although she will always choose a Buzz Lightyear outfit in preference to anything else.

It appeared that Jane's behaviour had several influences including those of popular culture (Dyson, 1997). Her brother is a role model, but most importantly she does not adhere to the dominant discourses of appropriate behaviour, clothes or toys for girls.

These children were in the minority: they were the ones who were observed crossing the boundaries of gender in their willingness to participate in a wide range of activities (Gallas, 1998; Thorne, 1993). Their behaviour had no effect on overall discourses within the class, perhaps because they were not actively counteracting the values of the discourse, as their parents did for them. Their influence was through passive role-modelling, which was not copied by the other children because they felt they held the most powerful discourse as the majority. The non-conformers were seen as 'not doing it right' and prompted responses from the other children to help them to 'get their gender behaviour right.'

The military context of the setting means frequently absent fathers and an imbalance of power between the careers of men and women in the community. The absence of fathers meant that the data has a female perspective. The imbalance of power in relation to work has affected the impact of parents as role models. The high incidence of women in low paid work is distorted by the overseas context, where two to three year tours mean that women barely have time to establish careers before they move on again. The transient nature of their lives means that women are more likely to accept low paid or voluntary work to occupy their time. In terms of the study, it alters the impact of parents as role models for children, fuelling the discourse that 'Daddy goes to work and Mummy looks after the children.', even though some of the individuals involved do not uphold these traditional views of gender roles.

At the start of this study, the reason that girls liked to draw and boys liked to build appeared to be that the discourses they subconsciously adhered to told them that this was what boys and girls do. The ways in which this message reached the children was complex. Through a combination of influences from parents, family, school, retailers and other members of their worlds, these messages were passed through to the children, who then actively reinforced them amongst their friends (Davies, 1994; Gallas, 1998; Graham, 1985). The gender discourses surrounding the children in this study were well-established and had been subconsciously affecting the lives of most of the participants for a long time. It is not possible to change their influence immediately, but the first step may be to raise awareness of their existence from the subconscious to the conscious (Davies, 1994). Those families who were raising their children as non-gender restricted individuals were also able to name and discuss these gender discourses – a first step towards challenging them.

Ethical dilemmas

In planning the project, I was well aware of the potentially controversial nature of my own feminist stance. In the three years I had lived and worked in the community, I had been struck by the imbalance of power within it and had been led to explore feminist theories as a result. On the outside, the community demonstrated a strong patriarchal hierarchy, composed of sub-divisions of class, culture and rank. There was a strong sense of military tradition amongst the families, many of them having several generations of military connections. In this milieu, I felt conscious of my own civilian, feminist, female status. This position raised ethical issues for me as researcher, considering whether my research could be conducted in partnership with participants, particularly parents, or if my own views would contaminate, or even offend them (Silverman, 2000).

From my feminist viewpoint, I had identified the issue of gender identity in the classroom, and I had to be prepared to make these known in order to engage in discussions with the participants, or ask them to validate my analysis of the data. Concealing my own stance in the project would also have limited access to validity through self-reflexive practices and would have detracted from the quality of the research, and, as Silverman (2000 p200) states: '...all research is contaminated to some extent by the values of the researcher. Only through those values do certain problems get identified and studied in particular ways'.

The potential for controversy recurred in the collection of data, which showed a high incidence of fathers showing strong emotional investment in their son's masculinity. Many fathers thought that deviance from the expected 'masculine' toys meant deviance from the norms of heterosexuality (Kehily, 2001). As Kehily (2001) argues, any deviance from the expected behaviour for boys may also suggest that the subject is deviating from the heterosexuality. In short, a common fear of the fathers was that boys who were experimenting with crossing gender borders (Thorne, 1993) were showing signs of being 'gay' (Kehily, 2001). In the military community, homosexuality was very much at odds with the dominant discourse and to suggest that cross-gender play might be beneficial to the boys had potential to cause conflict.

Niall's mother reported that when she bought dolls for her son to play with, she did so during her husband's deployment and not with his approval. Other mothers told similar stories of their sons crossing the boundaries of gender-specific toys while their fathers were away, because they 'didn't approve.'

Areas for further research

In the course of this research I found that many of the families had also lived in other military communities overseas. Some of the themes of this study would also be themes of parallel communities: the fathers' absence, the mothers' suspension of their careers and the patriarchal hierarchy of the military system. A comparable study of another military setting, or a contrasting civilian location, would provide an interesting parallel to this study and shed more light on the impact of gender-stereotypes on children's behaviour and development.

References
Aubrey, C, David, T, Godfrey, R and Thompson, L (2000) *Early childhood research: issues in methodology and ethics.* London: Routledge

Bogdan, R and Biklen, S (1998) *Qualitative research for education: An introduction to theory and methods.* London: Allyn and Bacon

Branthwaite, A (1985) The Development of social identity and self-concept' in Branthwaite, A and Rogers, D (eds) *Children growing up.* Milton Keynes: Open University Press

Davies, B (1994) *Poststructuralist theory and classroom practice.* Australia: Deakin University Press

Dyson, A H (1997) *Writing superheroes: contemporary childhood, popular culture and classroom literacy.* New York: Teachers College Press

Edwards, A (2001) Qualitative designs and analysis in MacNaughton, G Rolfe, S A and Siraj-Blatchford, I *Doing childhood research.* Buckingham: Open University Press

Francis, B (2001) 'Beyond postmodernism: feminist agency in educational research in Francis, B and Skelton, C (eds) *Investigating gender: contemporary perspectives in education.* Buckingham: Open University Press

Gallas, K (1998) *'Sometimes I can be anything': power, gender and identity in a primary classroom.* London: Teachers College Press

Gavey, N (1997) 'Feminist post-structuralism and discourse analysis' in Gergen, M and Davis, S. (eds) *Towards a new psychology of gender.* London: Routledge

Graham, H (1985) 'Psychosexual development' in Branthwaite, A and Rogers, D (eds) *Children growing up.* Milton Keynes: Open University Press

Grieshaber, S (2001) Equity issues in research design in MacNaughton, G, Rolfe, S A and Siraj-Blatchford, I. *Doing childhood research.* Buckingham: Open University Press

Kehily, M J (2001) Issues of gender and sexuality in schools, in Francis, B and Skelton, C (eds) *Investigating gender: contemporary perspectives in education.* Buckingham: Open University Press

Lowe, K (1998) 'Gendermaps' in Yelland, N (ed) *Gender in early childhood education.* London: Routledge

MacNaughton, G (1998) Improving our gender equity tools: a case for discourse analysis in Yelland, N (ed) *Gender in early childhood education.* London: Routledge

Maynard, M (1994) Methods, practice and epistemology: the debate about feminism and research in Maynard, M and Purvis, J (eds) *Researching women's' lives from a feminist perspective.* London: Taylor and Francis

Messner, M (2000) Barbie girls versus sea monsters: children constructing gender. *Gender and Society,* 14 (6) pp765-784

Minns, H (1985) Girls don't get holes in their clothes: sex typing in the primary school in NATE *Alice in genderland.* England: David Green Printers

Nichols, S (2002) Parents' construction of their children as gendered, literate subjects: a critical discourse analysis. *Journal of early childhood literacy,* 2 (2) pp 123- 144

Rolfe, S (2001) Direct observation in MacNaughton, G Rolfe, S A and Siraj-Blatchford, I. *Doing childhood research.* Buckingham: Open University Press

Silverman, D (2000) *Doing qualitative research: a practical handbook.* London: Sage Publications

Siraj-Blatchford, I and Siraj-Blatchford, J (2001) Surveys and questionnaires: an evaluative case study, in MacNaughton, G Rolfe, S A and Siraj-Blatchford, I *Doing childhood research.* Buckingham: Open University Press

Smith, M (1994) Putting gender on the agenda, in Frith, R and Mahoney, P (eds) *Promoting quality and equality in schools: empowering teachers through change.* London: David Fulton Publishers

Thorne, B (1993) *Gender play: girls and boys in school.* Buckingham: Open University Press

8

Seeing gender through
the eyes of young girls

Rachael Leslie

Introduction

A traditional children's rhyme from *Mother Goose* (Opie, 1996) is where the journey to 'seeing' gender began:

> What are little boys made of, made of,
> What are little boys made of?
> Snips and snails, and puppy-dogs' tails:
> That's what little boys are made of, made of.
> What are little girls made of, made of,
> What are little girls made of?
> Sugar and spice, and all things nice:
> That's what little girls are made of, made of.

Gender bias was a key area for study as I am a teacher in an all girls primary school. Gender has a particular impact on the children, teachers and the school when teaching in an all female environment without interaction with any male role models. The children in my class were immersed in female thinking, language, emotion and behaviour from their peers and the adults around them. The emphasis on 'being female' is undoubtedly strong and it was this perspective that particularly interested me. How did the girls in my class see their own female gender identity?

Studies of gender identity and young children make interesting reading (Francis, 1998; Davies, 1989; MacNaughton, 2000; Paechter, 2001). Paechter (2001 p49) refers to the 'private matter' of gender identity and

73

notes: 'we cannot take gender as simply given; we have constantly to perform our gender and to interpret the performances of others'. Similarly, Davies (1989 p229) observed that 'who one is, is always an open question with a shifting answer depending upon the positions made available within one's own and others' discursive practices'. This 'performing' of gender identity is where my research lay. It involved the five and six year-old girls in the class I was teaching at the time and took an ethnographic approach in that the children themselves carried out the research: it concentrated specifically on how they identified with their gender. I wanted to establish which people, places, objects and experiences were of special significance to them and, as Paechter (2001) commented, 'performed' their femaleness. As a focus for my study I posed the question 'what do girls see as symbols of their female gender identity'? The 'seeing' part of the research was adopted in almost a literal sense as I decided to give the children cameras to photograph the images they believed were important. I asked each girl to take twelve photographs of symbols of their gender identity. The children provided visual data in their role as photographers and from this data I carried out informal paired interviews with the girls about the images they chose. The final aspect of my study involved the girls creating individual books containing their photographs and personal comments about them.

Image-based research

Research involving children as the authors of photographs has recently come into its own (Schratz and Steiner-Loffler, 1998; DeMarie, 2001; Moss, 2001). Schratz and Steiner-Loffler (1998) investigated children's self-evaluation of primary school culture and were keen to find a research method which accounted for the 'pupil's perspective' (p236). The children photographed areas of the school they liked and disliked and followed this by compiling posters using the photos and comments to explain their choices. Schratz and Steiner-Loffler concluded (p249) that the children had produced 'powerful' images that contributed 'to making visible the invisible'. Moss (2001) researched literacy in the home and gave a group of seven and eight year-old children cameras to photograph any literacy-based events and resources that occurred. She also interviewed the children about the photographs they had taken to help establish the circumstances behind a picture and what else they might have wanted to include. Moss uncovered what I feel to be the essence of research involving children taking photographs: that their perceptions matter. Pink (2001) begins her chapter on visual ethnography with a statement of how powerful images are: 'they are inextricably interwoven with our personal identities, narratives, lifestyles, cultures and societies, as well as with definitions of history, space and truth' (p17). She acknowledges the intense role images play in our lives and in particular she touches on the special relationship that exists between the self and images.

Image-based research was appropriate for an investigation which had a visual focus. Like the girls I too wanted to 'see' what they identified with as signs of their female gender. To fulfil this I decided to equip them with cameras to take photographs of whatever objects, people, places and things they felt were special to them as girls. The children took a camera home with them for a weekend and returned it to school when they had finished photographing. The children provided visual data in their role as photographers from which I carried out informal, conversational interviews with pairs of children. We looked at their own set of prints and talked about what they had photographed, why they had taken a particular picture, what they liked/disliked about a picture and stories surrounding a photograph for example. After this informal interview they decided how they would like their pictures to appear in their book. At this point I acted as their scribe and wrote down what the children wanted to say about each picture. These comments were then typed out and added to the pictures. When the books were completed we looked at the books as a class activity before each girl took it home to share with her family and others.

The children as photographers

The setting for my investigation is the school where I currently work in a city in the north of England. It is a small independent school for girls (120 children in total) with seven classes of children aged from four to twelve years old. A class of eighteen five and six year-old girls took part in the research. I first discussed the project with the children at the beginning of May and planned to send the cameras home over two weekends before the Spring Bank holiday. Their initial response was enthusiastic and full of questions and statements such as 'can I take a picture of my stone collection?' and 'I'm going to take a picture of my rabbit'. We talked about what pictures they intended taking and I reiterated that my focus for the investigation was my interest in each one of the girls and in what mattered to them. The issue of 'what to do' with the photos arose during this discussion and one suggestion of putting them in a book sparked the idea for the individual 'my special things book', which would include the children's photographs and words. The ownership of the photographs became clear. It was decided that we could all look at each other's books and I would be able to borrow them over the summer, with the assurance I would return them to the girls when I had finished.

As all eighteen children were involved I decided twelve photographs per child would provide enough material for analysis. Asking the children to think about twelve 'things' seemed a manageable number for them, and as one standard 24 exposure film could therefore be used by two children, the potential of 216 photographs would be sufficient data. The idea was for one girl to use the camera first and take twelve pictures, then return it to school for someone else to take the final twelve pictures. I had a final general discussion with the girls to answer any questions and worries they still had. We looked at one of the cameras and talked about how to take a picture and they could have a practice try if they wanted to. I again stressed the ownership of the task: that it was to be *their* decision as to what to photograph so long as it fitted the 'special to me' criteria. I was keen to achieve parental support for the task; if the parents took an interest they might offer technical support or allay a sudden urge to take twelve pictures of the inside of the car! However, there was a strict 'no grown ups allowed' rule when it came to the identification and taking of the photographs.

It took a full two weeks before all the cameras were returned with the photo-task completed. Until a film is processed there is no assurance that the task has been a success – do the photographs actually exist and are they clear? For example Millie photographed her mum and dad sitting near a window in the living room. The flash seems not to have worked, creating only a silhouette of their figures. Millie's comment was 'this photograph didn't come out very well but it doesn't matter. I love my Mummy and Daddy'.

When the children returned the cameras some liked showing me what they had photographed and talked through the record card of pictures they had kept. The films were developed over the half-term holiday and were available for discussion when the girls came back to school. I decided to work with two children at a time looking at their set of photographs and discussing the images they had taken. I used non-contact time and lunch breaks to keep interruptions to a minimum and devote time for the children to look at and talk about their pictures while I made notes. Often the children talked freely about why they had taken a picture or what they had photographed. They chatted about each other's photos and I frequently heard the comment 'oh I've got one like that too!' when a photograph of mum, dad, pets or toys was identified. Sometimes I asked a question about the content or context of a photograph, to establish the background of a picture or clarify what a particular object or image was.

I noted relevant information about pictures. Many were easily identifiable, such as members of the family, scooters, books, school friends or jewellery. Other pictures had a different meaning from what they appeared to show: Paige took a picture of a snail on a wall because 'I like things to do with the outside'. Some photographs were difficult to identify because of poor lighting and a few were not of what was intended: Kate had a photograph of the living-room wall when it should have been of her sister Lucy! Young children taking photographs within a research context has its difficulties but there are rewards. Photography carries risks such as technical failure, but these are not problems exclusive to child photographers. I was impressed with how the children handled the cameras in terms of both the quality and quantity of the images. Out of potentially 216 pictures, 209 were developed. Ten girls successfully took twelve photographs, two girls took thirteen pictures and the other six girls took between nine and eleven.

Understanding the photographs
Using photographs was successful. The images provided a personal, meaningful and honest representation of the girls' perceptions, as viewed through a very powerful lens: their own interpretation. Interviewing them about their pictures was crucial to the study. Harden *et al* (2000 p4) discuss the merits of children using photography within a research context providing 'they are utilised as an occasion or stimulus for talk rather than as evidence in their own right'.

Analysing the children's photographs was difficult and my initial task was how to organise them. Taking a qualitative approach, I coded each picture according to the subject matter or content. I grouped similar subjects into a category so as to manage the data and make it more accessible. To code and organise the photographs into workable data, I used my understanding of the children's photographs and their own interpretations of these pictures as honestly as possible, and in that sense I feel this justified and, in a sense, corroborated, my decision to analyse the photos thus.

What the children photographed
Davies (1993 p22) talked of the 'interaction between oneself and others' as central to most theories of identity. This was reflected overall in the girls' photographs of adults and children. Siblings and parents were the

most frequently photographed, totalling over a quarter of the photos. Pictures of grandparents, other adults, friends, school friends and self-portraits contributed to 'people' being the most frequently photographed subject; 85 photographs were of people, over one third of those taken.

The children's focus on family, adults and children echoes Paechter's thinking that to understand who we are we need to have some sense of who we are not. Paechter (2001) believes this process begins early on in a child's life and is developed and reinforced through social interaction. Many of the children's photographs were connected with social activities and interaction, 'Rainbow' guides, dancing and swimming were photographed eight times. The emphasis on being social was also represented by seventeen pictures of school friends and other friends – both girls and boys.

Francis (1998) and Lloyd and Duveen (1992) talk of the importance of 'visual signs' of gender in constructing our gender identity. Clothes and gender-stereotyped accessories are, as Francis (1998 p33) notes, what children 'take up' as 'signifiers of their gender allegiance'. I looked at three such 'visual signs': clothes, jewellery and make-up, to see what particular impact if any, they had on the total number of photographs. Five photographs of clothes were taken, three of jewellery and one picture of make-up. The five photographs of clothes included two bridesmaid dresses, a 'favourite' dress and two school uniforms (perhaps signifying the female environment of the girls' school). A total of nine pictures were, as Francis (1998) comments, 'signifiers' of their gender. This is a surprisingly low figure in relation to the total, clothes and jewellery could have been expected to feature more significantly.

The photographic data and individual conversations with the children indicated that the children 'see' people as symbols of the their female gender identity. Relationships appeared important to the girls. People, including family members, friends and other adults were represented in all the girls' photographs and social influences were definitely important signifiers of the girls' identity. Paechter (2001 p49) discusses how we have to 'perform' our gender identity constantly – perhaps the children's photographs of people is a reflection of the adults and children to whom they 'perform' their gender identity most often.

Social influence, such as the people to whom we are most connected, is embedded in the complex process of constructing a gender identity. People and relationships permeate all aspects of our lives and this influence was evident in the children's decision to photograph family and friends. Our sense of who we are is constantly reinforced by the people who matter to us, and what the children represented through their photographs was the people who mattered to them. 'Performing' our gender is an active process which Davies (1993) believes is an ongoing and changing process. She believes children must have the ability 'to read and interpret the landscape of the social world' (p17). The popularity of photographs representing the girl's family, school friends and their hobbies were perhaps evidence of how they interpreted this 'landscape'.

As signs of their gender, identity toys and play equipment were second in popularity as a subject. I expected the type of toys the children photographed would reflect current trends such as Beanie Babies, Harry Potter memorabilia and Barbie dolls but this was not the case. Indeed the only toys photographed often enough to become a subject in their own right were teddies and dolls and only two were Barbie dolls. Perhaps this indicates that although the girls may own these current play commodities they attach less importance to them just because they are current. Unlike people, they can be easily acquired and disposed of.

The girls were making quite a bold statement here. Media and peer pressure to take up current trends and fashions can be overwhelming. So their decision to ignore this pressure in favour of photographing real people shows independent thinking. It could be argued that parents were influential in deciding what and who to photograph but there were too many commonalities across the children's photographs for them to have been a major influence. The common theme of photographing family members was evident in the girls' photographs and this created a significant dilemma. Possibly the children did not interpret the task as I had hoped they would, in that they photographed things that were special to them, and not necessarily because they represented their gender identity. I believe that what they photographed had special meaning for them, and that the photographs reflected, and to an extent represented, their identity. But I am not totally satisfied that their photographs are indeed symbols of their gender identity. However, it could be argued that gender identity is embedded in the concept of identity, in which case the girls' photographs are indeed symbols of their gender identity. A comparative study with boys would be needed to answer this question.

The books the girls created contained personal photographs and thoughts on the things that were special to them as girls. These images and their interpretation of them were central to my investigation. The children were enthusiastic research participants. I am grateful for their honest participation and hope that this is reflected in my understanding of their photographs. The children quite clearly demonstrated their own perspective so it seems right to illustrate this as truthfully as possible: through the girls' eyes.

The photographs
Paige's photographs

All the girls who participated in my research provided a unique account of their innermost thoughts and feelings culminating in eighteen 'special' books. Paige's story is perhaps most illustrative of my study as her photographs echo subjects other girls chose yet they also possess an individual quality. There are few gender-stereotyped images. Paige's pictures do not have a particularly 'girly' feel. Below are extracts from the interview with Paige about the pictures she had taken.

Looking through her photographs Paige said:

> This is my egg cup. It's on the coffee table. We haven't got that coffee table anymore! I made that out of plasticine. I got a piece and flattened it out then I got another bit and rolled it like a tube and stuck it on the top. I made it at home.
>
> This is my Lego model boat. It's my favourite boat. It took about an hour to make. Look it's on the same coffee table! I've got horses as well you know. You can see the tail of the horse [points to photo] and that brown bit there is the ear of another one.
>
> It's my plant – it's a special thing. It's got two flowers in. I like things to do with the garden.

Figure 8.1: Ah! That's my S Club 7 CD. It's my favourite CD. Can you see the chess thing in the background (points at photo)? Daddy's the expert! I play with mummy sometimes. I've got loads of CDs... I like dancing to them.

Figure 8.2: This is Pandora and my other toys but I've got loads more! I've got 177 toys. I got Pandora on Christmas Day, she had a biscuit round her neck that said 'eat me' but I didn't get any taller. That's Brown-steps (points to photo). Grandma gave me hers to borrow but I accidently kept her!! And that's Flopsy the rabbit – she's had lots of adventures you know. I've lost her in Debenhams or maybe it was Boots.

> This is my seaside. It's on the same coffee table. I got all those things from the seaside. I got some from Cornwall and from lots of different beaches.
>
> This is a snail on my wall. I like things to do with the outside. I thought it was a lump at first!
>
> This is mummy with daddy's face as well!
>
> Ah, this is daddy at the train station. He was going to London you know.

What I found so powerful from Paige's and other images is the children's ability to see, represent and interpret their own worlds with such clarity and meaning. What the cameras gave the children was not only an alternative way of seeing themselves but also a new way of looking at themselves. The photographs enabled them to look beyond the surface interpretations of the pictures, as in this conversation I had with Isobel about a photograph of her school shoes:

> These are my old school shoes. I keep them in a box under the cupboard and I've had them for a year and a half. I don't want to throw them out because I got them when I started school and I like them. They're all scruffy because mummy never cleaned them and I like these shoes better now because they've got heels on and I'm older now.

Figure 8.3: Those are my tap shoes. They're size 12. I have dancing lessons. I love dancing.

Seeing ahead

Studies of at how children construct their gender identity (Davies, 1993; Jones, 1996; Francis, 1988; MacNaughton, 2000) have emphasised thinking that this is an active process. They view gender identity not as a given but as something that can shift and change within life. As Francis (1998 p8) comments 'gender is not fixed but rather that we are positioned and position ourselves in gender discourse'. Where I could not draw a conclusion from my investigation was over this shifting aspect of the girls' gender identity. The photographs offered valuable insights into what they identified as important to them, but these images were very much static images that did not illustrate this positioning. The photographs represented the children's thinking *at that time* and helped me to construct the girls' gender identity. They represented the significance of family, friends and social activity on the whole process of self-identity.

I see potential for further research focusing on this shifting nature of gender identity. It would be interesting to initiate a similar image-based investigation with the same girls later in their lives. Looking back at the symbols they chose to represent as signifiers of their gender identity may help to establish where they have positioned themselves within gender discourses. Although my study did not set out to compare genders, to have observed what boys of the same age photographed and used these alongside the girls' pictures, could perhaps have made a clearer distinction between what was photographed because it was simply important to the girls. My investigation began with the traditional rhyme 'what are little boys made of'. I expected the girls' photographs to have led me down a soft, pink path but I was quite wrong. They demonstrated that they were independent thinkers, with a strong sense of their own being, although I did indeed observe puppy-dogs' tails, a little sugar and spice, quite a few things nice and even the odd snail!

References

Davies, B. (1989) *Frogs and Snails and Feminist Tails*. Preschool Children and Gender. London: Allen and Unwin

Davies, B. (1993) *Shards of Glass. Children reading and writing beyond gendered identities.* New Jersey: Hampton Press Inc

DeMarie, D. (2001) 'A Trip to the Zoo: Children's Words and Photographs' *Early Childhood Research and Practice* 3 (1) pp.1-26 http://ecrp.uiuc.edu/v3nl/demarie.html

Francis, B. (1998) *Power Plays. Primary School Children's Constructions of Gender, Power and Adult Work.* Staffordshire: Trentham Books Limited

Harden, J., Scott, S., Backett-Milburn, K. and Jackson, S. (2000) 'Can't talk won't talk?: Methodological issues in researching children' *Sociological Research Online*, 5 (2) http://www.socresonline.org.uk/5/2/harden.html

Jones, L. (1996) 'Young girls' notions of femininity' *Gender and Education* 8 (3) pp. 311-321

Lloyd, B. and Duveen, G. (1992) *Gender Identities and Education. The Impact of Starting School.* Hertfordshire: Harvester Wheatsheaf

MacNaughton, G. (2000) *Rethinking Gender in Early Childhood Education.* London: Paul Chapman Publishing Ltd

Moss, G. (2001) 'Seeing with the camera: analysing children's photographs of literacy in the home' *Journal of Research in Reading* 24 (3) pp. 279-292

Opie, I. (ed) (1996) *My very first Mother Goose.* London: Walker Books

Paechter, C. (2001) 'Using poststructuralist ideas in gender theory and research' in B. Francis and C. Skelton (eds) *Investigating Gender. Contemporary Perspectives in Education.* Buckingham: Open University Press pp. 41-51

Pink, S. (2001) *Doing Visual Ethnography. Images, Media and Representation in Research.* London: SAGE Publications Ltd

Schratz, M. and Steiner-Loffler, U. (1998) 'Pupils using photographs in school self-evaluation' in J. Prosser (ed) *Image-based Research A Sourcebook for Qualitative Researchers.* London: Falmer Press pp.235-251

9

Imogen's story: inclusion in a mainstream school in Dubai

Louise Short

The Context

Since 1993 in the UK the general principle has applied that children with special educational needs (SEN) should normally be educated at mainstream schools if this is what the parents want. This was enshrined in the Education Act 1996. Subsequent ratification of this principle at the UNESCO world conference in Salamanca, in 1994, has undoubtedly influenced the literature on the philosophy and practice of inclusive education. In 1997 the then new Labour Government set out a strategy to improve standards for pupils with special educational needs (DfEE, 1997). A clear commitment to promoting greater inclusion was signalled and the significant educational, social and moral benefits of this policy were highlighted. A later review of the statutory framework for inclusion (DfEE, 1998), in conjunction with the Disability Rights Task Force, ultimately strengthened the rights of children with statements of special educational needs to a place in a mainstream school.

In 1998, I started working with a colleague whose little girl, Imogen, has cerebral palsy. Her daughter was due to start a mainstream primary school in Dubai, where we were working as learning support teachers. This chapter records my interest both personal and professional in the development of Imogen's education experience in a mainstream British

Curriculum primary school. Private schools in Dubai exist outside the auspices of UK Government funding or initiatives, but Imogen's school proudly wears the mantle of a 'British Curriculum' establishment and to this extent it is influenced by current educational theory and British educational practice.

The issues that have always interested me were my first point of reference:

■ What is the history behind Imogen's inclusion?

■ How is Imogen disabled?

■ What do people think about children with special needs in mainstream schools?

■ What does Imogen herself think of her education experience?

■ Is Imogen successfully included in her school?

These questions underpinned my methodological approach. Interviews, observations and documentary evidence and a review of the literature built up Imogen's 'case'.

Defining terms of inclusion

John O'Neill (1996) writes:

> Special Educational Needs provision tends to be one of the more complex, least understood and most volatile elements of the educational periodic table. (O'Neill, 1996 p9)

The terms 'inclusion' and 'integration' are often used interchangeably, which causes confusion. Farrell (1997), cites official papers such as *Excellence for all children: meeting special educational needs* (DfEE, 1997), which stated that the Labour government supports the principle of inclusive and integrated education. However, most researchers in the field now agree that the two words 'inclusion' and 'integration' are no longer synonymous but are points on a continuum from 'segregation to inclusion' (Clough, 1998).

The Centre for Studies on Inclusive Education (CSIE, 1989) uses the term 'inclusion' to reflect new understanding of this philosophy. They say that integration may be construed as something done to disabled people by non-disabled people, according to their standards and conditions. However inclusion conveys more clearly a right to belong to the mainstream and is a joint undertaking to end discrimination and towards equal opportunities for all children.

Ainscow (1995) advocates the creation of 'inclusive schools for all', 'where the aim is to restructure schools in order to respond to the needs of all children'. However, this utopian view is not without its critics. Wilson (1999) challenges Ainscow:

> When Ainscow writes, *'Pupils are entitled to take part in all subjects and activities,'* it is hard to know what he is actually saying. Suppose the activity is playing Beethoven or doing quadratic equations. Is he saying there should be no administrative barrier which should prevent pupils from doing so? This of course is absurd. (Wilson,1999 p111)

The 1981 Education Act stated that a pupil was seen as having special educational needs if they have:

> ...a significantly greater difficulty in learning than the majority of children his (sic) age or has a disability which hinders or prevents him from making use of educational facilities of a kind generally provided. (HMSO, 1981)

This theme of relativity when defining SEN is echoed more recently by Clough (1998), who states:

> As a semi-technical term, Special Educational Needs refers generally to those who have more, and more significant, difficulty than their peers. ...the whole drive in developments in thinking about SEN is toward a relative understanding of learning difficulty: just as all learners have strengths and weaknesses, so does each teacher, so do schools and colleges they work in and so do the curricula they provide. Thus, a child who appears to be 'failing' in one particular class, subject or school might be expected to perform very differently in another class, subject or school. This is to say that there are no absolute measures of special educational need, but that a judgement about learning difficulty must always be relative to the total learning context in which difficulty is perceived or experienced. ...it is an important function of the definition that learning difficulties occur – with greater or lesser severity – *at all levels of an educational system.* (Clough, 1998 p5)

Whilst the concept of a spectrum of difficulty is easy to visualise and there is agreement about the pupils at one end of the spectrum having special educational needs, it is harder to determine where to draw the line between these pupils and those with so-called 'normal' developmental needs. If we apply the definition to Imogen, there is no doubt that she has serious physical difficulties, which would place her at one end of the spectrum but her academic performance is better than several of her peers. Does this mean that she moves along the spectrum? Can we label her as having SEN if she outperforms her classmates? If she is put into a larger class does this combined effect increase her rating on the spectrum and make her more deserving of the title 'special needs' than her peers who are also being disadvantaged?

My own view of Imogen's needs depends upon how I view her in relation to my own value systems. They are influenced by legislation and my sense of what is right and appropriate, according to my own experience. These ideas are socially constructed and may therefore be different from those of others. The important point is that we all have our own ideas about what constitutes 'special' in educational needs.

Through interviewing the people directly involved in Imogen's learning – her parents, teachers, physiotherapist and Imogen herself – I was able to build up a detailed picture of her educational experience.

Interviewing Imogen

Processes of interviewing adults are well documented, but finding out Imogen's own views raised ethical issues which needed some thought.

There is growing recognition of the importance of listening to children's views and of incorporating children's views in research. Christensen and James (2000) suggest that special methods are not necessary for research with children, who can take part in both structured and unstructured interviews. Critchley (2001) advises that interviews be short and focused.

Imogen's interview experience was both enjoyable and informative. I had decided previously to invite another child, Sophie, to join her in an activity and interview them together while they were busy. Holmes (1998) found that the strategy of interviewing children while they were drawing was successful, the idea being that because they were occupied and would not become bored with the interview process. I found it worked well. The girls are great friends and I thought the conversation might flow more freely if they were playing together.

Imogen is seven and Sophie nearly five. They were very excited about being taped. I explained that I wanted to find out more about them and that I would ask them some questions. Both girls seemed to take the interview experience completely in their stride. I have taught Imogen in the past and I have a good relationship with her. The girls continued their colouring activity throughout the interview and giggled sometimes. Both girls answered all the questions clearly and Imogen asked me a few times if 'it was alright to say this', which indicated that she was confident enough in the process to ask for clarification.

Including Imogen

Imogen's educational experience is good. Each of the professionals I interviewed approached their interview thoughtfully and showed an in-depth knowledge and sensitivity towards their pupil. All thought Imogen's inclusion in the school was successful. The school has tried hard to provide for her special needs. For example, they have made costly structural changes to buildings to improve access.

Imogen is a happy, confident child, who is generally well-motivated and comes to school willingly. She moves around readily, she has physical access to all areas of the campus and plays her part in the life of the school, along with classmates. She has many friends, and has an active out-of-school schedule, which keeps both of her parents very busy.

She needs very little physical help on a daily basis, and gets some academic help, but no more and often less than many of her peers. She is able to access most of the set curriculum and is certainly achieving. Analysis of the Access to the National Curriculum Checklist (Reception – Year 2), highlights the only area of concern as being the length of time it takes her to complete some, not all, written tasks. The Physical Education curriculum is not directly referred to, therefore her profile is strong. Her success is due to the unquestionable hard work of her teachers, but her inclusion is almost by accident, rather than by design.

Imogen is expected to fit into the curriculum, rather than the curriculum being adapted to meet her needs. There is no formal vehicle for inter-agency support and a heavy reliance on her mother by the school, to oversee her physical development and act as chief liaison officer between the Therapy Centre and the school. Thus, despite the school's obvious success with Imogen as an individual 'case', her inclusion is co-incidental. There is no real philosophy of inclusion, nor established policy of inclusion in the school. In short, Imogen has been 'integrated' rather than 'included'.

Imogen's education experience in a mainstream school is considered to be a success because she is so remarkably able to fit in to the practices established for the majority. She doesn't require anything extra, in the eyes of the school, other than what is currently provided for her. Because she can conform to the general requirements of the majority of non-disabled students and because she is an able child in that she has academic potential beyond some of her peers, she does not stand out as being different.

There is no evidence to suggest that any other child with cerebral palsy, or any special educational need, would be able to benefit from an education at her school because there is no formal inclusion policy. The context is important here. Dubai is a young modern city. Forty years ago, there were no formal schools at all. The pace of change has been rapid – but schools following the British Curriculum operate somewhat in a vacuum, with virtually no external pressure to conform to current British practices. Decisions are often left to individual headteachers, who are answerable to a board of governors – made up of influential businessmen, not educationists.

Local culture has highlighted how far it has to go in its understanding of Special Needs Education by publishing an article in the local press entitled: 'Man with Special Needs gets good job!' This thinking adds to the responsibility of individuals in schools like Imogen's. Policy decisions will help to fashion not only the school's philosophy and practice but also that of the community as a whole.

I was told that when Imogen started in the nursery class at the Therapy Centre there were five children in her group. All of them attended mainstream nurseries. Imogen is the only one at a mainstream primary school. However, as Imogen is the only disabled child at the school, she can be singled out as being different because there are no others like her in the mainstream. When asked: 'How do you feel ... that you're the only one that's got a walker?'. Imogen replied, 'Yes, It's a little bit lonely... sad sometimes, not sad but lonely.'

We should not underestimate the gulf between writing about special needs and actually living with them. This chapter is a snapshot of the education experience of a child with a life-long disability. As Pereera (2001) confirms, personal views and values are developed and evolve through individual experiences and so life experiences may change perspectives.

In schools like Imogen's, in Dubai, the move away from the old equal opportunities model towards practices requiring more accountability has been gathering momentum. There is accountability at an academic level and the next goal is to achieve accountability at a social level.

Conclusion: developing inclusive education

An essential element to understanding the philosophy of inclusion is recognising the fundamental difference between two terms. Stainback and Stainback (1990) claim that integration expects students to change or be 'supported' to fit into the school. Inclusion, on the contrary, expects the school to change to suit the child. This must be the focus for change

Branson and Miller argue that:

> ...integration must be... programme-oriented towards its own destruction, aiming to destroy the very categories which are seen as needing to be 'integrated' into the 'normal' world. If the disabled are 'normal', so much as an accepted part of our world that we take their presence,

their humanity, their special qualities for granted, then there can be no integration, for there is no segregation, either conceptually... or actually. (Branson and Miller, 1989 p48)

References

Ainscow, M. (1995) 'Education For All: making it happen'. Keynote address: International Special Education Congress, Birmingham, July in *Inclusive Schooling* NSIN Research Matters No. 14, Summer 2001, p2

Branson, J. and Miller, L, (1989) Inclusion or Integration? in Slee, R. *Is There a Desk With My Name on It?* London: The Falmer Press

Christensen, P. and James, A. (eds) (2000) *Research with Children: Perspectives and Practices*, London: Falmer Press

Clough, P. (1998) *Managing inclusive education: from policy to practice*, London: Paul Sage Publishing

Critchley, D. (2001) Children's Assessment of their own Learning in Clough, P. and Nutbrown, C. (eds) (2001) *Voices of Arabia; Essays in Educational Research*, Sheffield: The University of Sheffield Press

Department for Education and Employment (DfEE) (1997) *Excellence for all children: meeting special educational needs*, London: HMSO

Department for Education and Employment (DfEE) (1998) *Meeting special educational needs: a programme for action*, London: HMSO

Farrell, M. (1997) *Teaching Pupils with Learning Difficulties: Strategies and Solutions*, London: Cassell

Her Majesty's Stationery Office (1981) *The Education Act 1981*. London: HMSO

Holmes, R. (1998) *Fieldwork with young children.* London: Sage

O'Neill, J. (1996) *Educational Management Development Unit Managing Special Needs in Schools*. Leicester: University of Leicester Press

Pereera, S (2001) Living with 'Special Educational Needs': mothers' perspectives in Clough, P. and Nutbrown, C. *Voices of Arabia, Essays in Educational Research*. Sheffield: University of Sheffield

Stainback, S. and Stainback, W. (1990) *Support Networking For Inclusive Schooling*. Baltimore, Md, Paul H. Brookes

Wilson, J. (1999) Some contextual difficulties about 'inclusion'. *Support for Learning* No.14 (3)

Part 3
ADULTS' INFLUENCES ON CHILDREN'S LEARNING

10

Working with children under three: the perspectives of three UK academics

Jools Page

Introduction

Neuroscience suggests that babies are born pre-programmed and ready to learn, suggesting that children's earliest experiences and relationships are paramount. There is strong evidence to suggest that highly skilled staff are required to care for babies and to cope with the highly complex triangular relationships between staff, children and parents. Work with children under three is an area which has largely been neglected. This chapter reports the views of three leading UK academics, Professor Lesley Abbott, Professor Tricia David and Peter Elfer. I am grateful to them for sharing their views.

Context and issues for provision for children under three in the UK

I have worked in the childcare sector for over twenty years, both caring for children and in policy-making roles. As a nursery nurse and later as a nursery manager, I enjoyed the hands-on care of children. As an early years lecturer, member and former chair of the county's Early Years Development and Childcare Partnership and most recently as a local authority government officer, I have gained insight into some of the issues and views that influence the childcare sector. Throughout this time my interest in the youngest children, those under three, has never wavered.

When, in 1986, I became a nursery nurse at a workplace day nursery, my interest in this age group intensified. My post involved working with the three to five year olds and although I enjoyed my work, I often took the opportunity to visit the children at the lower age group of the nursery. On occasions, I voiced my desire to change the age group that I worked with but was informed by my line manager, who intended it as a compliment, that my skills would be 'wasted' with the babies. This was a concept I found difficult to understand but naively accepted. Linden (2000) suggests that it is a view commonly held by those who do not work with children under three.

> Practitioners who work with the under threes are sometimes irritated by the view of colleagues that they have the easier or less interesting part of work with young children. (Lindon, 2000 p19)

I can recall my concern about the lack of observation and checking procedures on sleeping babies who were placed in their prams at the bottom of the garden. I volunteered to work over lunch time to keep a watchful eye on the sleeping toddlers, who would wake and try to sit up, but get caught up in their pram harnesses. My colleagues were always busy and worked very hard, trying to keep up with the increasing demands of the smallest and most vulnerable children in their care. However, I always felt uneasy about aspects of their care and that something was missing, although, at the time, I was not sure what that something was.

Children under three: issues from the literature
Brain studies
According to recent scientific research, babies and young children are born with the capacity to understand far more than was previously thought to be the case. 'We've learned more in the last thirty years about what babies and young children know than we did in the preceding 2,500 years' (Gopnik, Meltzoff and Kuhl, 1999 p22). Not long ago we were told that newborn babies do not feel pain, or that young children find it impossible to see the world from anything but their own perspective (David, 1999 p87). This view has now been challenged by new scientific research, based on recent observational studies of babies, using video cameras. 'By using videotape we can objectively measure what babies do and look at it slowly, over and over' (Gopnik, Meltzoff and Kuhl, 1999 p21), building on the successful observational methods of earlier scientists such as Vygotsky and Piaget, despite the differences in their theoretical approach.

Scientists have challenged the long-held view that babies cannot distinguish one human face from another, and suggest that they know more than was originally thought from the moment they are born. Experiments have been carried out to discover if babies get bored, if they can recognise faces and if they can differentiate between objects. By video-recording newborn babies in controlled situations, an independent observer can observe such things as eye movements and analyse them to see which pictures babies prefer. Experiments such as these have produced startling evidence suggesting that babies can recognise different faces within a few days of birth. The process, called 'habituation' (Gopnik, Meltzoff and Kuhl, p27; Brierley, 1994 p81), seeks to confirm the need for novelty and stimulation. 'The brain thrives on variety and stimulation. Monotony of surroundings, toys that only do one thing are soon disregarded by the brain' (Brierley, 1994 p82). Similar experiments have been carried out to establish the levels of understanding that babies and young children have throughout the first three years of their life, the hypotheses being that children are born with these innate tendencies and that adults are required to harness and support those skills, in order for children to continue their educational path in a learning environment.

Attachment theories

Recent brain studies have challenged many previous theories about babies and young children's capacity to think and have sought to build on previous theories of the importance of the role of the main adult or carer, which is in most cases the mother. In 1953 John Bowlby argued, in his famous study, *Child Care and the Growth of Love* (Bowlby, 1965), that infants form a relationship with their mother which is special and different from the relationships they form with others. He described this process as 'monotropy', similar to 'imprinting'. He went on to suggest that the bond between mother and infant in the first six months is so intense that if broken, this will cause irreparable damage to the infant. Bowlby's theory was at its height as servicemen were returning from the second world war and jobs, which had been largely carried out by women during the war years, were needed for the men. Bowlby's study became the object of political debate and was used by post-war pressure groups to argue that women should stay at home to rear their young. It was suggested that not to do so would have long-lasting damaging effects on the infants. However, Bowlby later argued that his earlier work had been misinterpreted and that his theory had been misunderstood.

> It has sometimes been alleged that I have expressed the view that
> mothering should always be provided by a child's natural mother, and

also that mothering 'cannot be safely distributed among several
figures' (Mead, 1962). No such views have been expressed by me.
(Bowlby, 1969 p303)

Bowlby's theory that children attach themselves to one main figure has
often been debated. Rutter (1972), for example, suggests infants can
form multiple attachments and concludes:

> If the mothering is of high quality and is provided by figures who re-
> main the same during the child's early life, then (at least up to four or
> five mother figures) multiple mothering need have no adverse affects.
> (Rutter, 1972 p25)

Rutter believes that when the mother goes out to work, the child is unlikely to suffer, provided the multiple relationships made with the child
are stable and good childcare is provided.

The interpretation of Bowlby's controversial theory has been argued and
debated for many years since its publication in the 1950s, and has fuelled
the on-going controversy about day care for children. Much of the
criticism surrounds the group on which Bowlby based his research: children who had been reared in residential institutions or separated from
their parents for long periods in hospital. Other critics of attachment
theory claim that secure attachment is not always necessary for healthy
development and may depend on cultural child-rearing practices
(Hennessy, Martin, Moss and Melhuish, 1992).

The impact of policy change

Profound changes in the lives of young children in the past thirty to forty
years have had a significant impact on the way in which children are
cared for and learn, both in and out of the home setting. Reasons for
change can be attributed to a number of factors: change in family
patterns; life changes in response to employment, particularly the increase in women returning to work and study; increased demand for
childcare; increase in ethnic diversity and Central Government direc-
tives, including legislative changes.

The 1989 Children Act (DoH, 1991) (superseding The 1948 Nurseries
and Childminders Regulation Act (DES, 1948) caused the most dramatic
change when it came into effect in 1991. It provided a new regulatory
and inspection framework for social services and private and voluntary
sector provision for children under the age of eight. Other recent legislation has focused on the needs of children over the age of three. The
Education Reform Act (HMSO, 1988), for example, introduced a
national curriculum for children of five years and over, and the Rumbold
Report (DfEE, 1990) looked at the educational experiences offered to

children aged three and four, although it did make reference to children under three. The Nursery and Grant – Maintained Schools Act (DfEE, 1996) gave the Office for Standards in Education (Ofsted) the power to inspect the quality of learning in early years settings.

In 1998 new Labour Prime Minister Tony Blair launched The National Childcare Strategy in response to the Green Paper *Meeting the Childcare Challenge* (DfEE, 1998). The strategy set out four key areas that required attention with regard to early education and childcare in England: Quality of childcare; affordability of childcare; availability of childcare and diversity of childcare.

The government began by giving additional responsibility to the already existing Early Years Development Partnerships to embrace childcare services as well. The Early Years Development and Childcare Partnerships (EYDCPs) were assembled from multi-agency groups in every local education authority (LEA) in England. Their remit was to take forward, at a local level, the government's vision for childcare and education for children aged from birth to fourteen years (up to sixteen years for children with special educational needs). Each EYDCP is charged with producing an annual plan to show how, through Government initiatives, countywide services will be delivered to meet the early years and childcare needs of the local community. In his foreword, Tony Blair stated that childcare in the UK had been 'neglected for too long'. He promised to address regulation of day care services, quality of registered provision and to develop a framework of qualifications for those working in the sector. During the consultation period responses were documented about the government's proposals. Respondents expressed their anxiety about whether under threes were being cared for satisfactorily within appropriate group care. Clear guidelines should be drawn up to ensure that the care provided was appropriate to the age and stage of the child. (DfEE, 1998, p4). In addition, whilst 'free' educational places for three and four year olds were welcomed, concern about the rise in costs for baby places was highlighted. An Early Excellence Centre (DfEE, 1997) programme was set up in 1997 to develop models of good practice through a range of services designed to meet the local needs of communities. In addition, in their 1998 spending review the government introduced Sure Start (DfEE, 1998), an early intervention programme for under fours in areas of high deprivation in the UK.

Ministers recognised that increasing the number of early years and childcare places depended on having: 'a highly skilled workforce' and that 'working with children is a demanding, skilled profession' (DfEE, 1999 p1). A high-level recruitment campaign was launched to raise the profile of careers in early years and play work. However, despite the access to free training, introduction of the minimum wage and the adoption of the European working time directive, the government still failed to recognise and address the issue of the poor pay and conditions of staff working with children in early years and childcare settings up and down the country.

Links to research in other disciplines

Are status and pay the only reasons for high staff turnover, particularly in day nurseries? Could it also be that anxiety about the relationships practitioners make with children has an impact on the retention of staff? Menzies-Lyth (1959), a psychoanalyst, identified the reasons for a high turnover of staff in a general hospital. She found that nursing staff were discouraged from forming any kind of close relationship with patients, despite having to perform intimate care and encouraged to keep busy with the day-to-day running of the ward. Relatives of the patients were found to resent the nurses and envy their caring skills. The nursing staff were expected to remain detached: it was considered unprofessional to form a relationship with a patient, beyond what was necessary. The study suggests that this factor could be linked to high staff turnover. Nurses complained that lack of support from their superiors left them feeling angry and resentful. By keeping the nursing staff busy, in an attempt to evade anxiety, the problem was exacerbated. Where staff were allowed to 'special' a patient who was extremely ill, the nurses reported emotions such as excitement and pleasure. In the main however, this practice was not invited. Menzies-Lyth (1988) observed that: 'The implied disregard of her own needs and capacities is distressing to the nurse; she feels she does not matter and no one cares what happens to her' (p71).

Further research suggests that children cared for in good quality settings benefit from early education and childcare, thus contesting earlier theories of emotional attachment (Moss and Melhuish, 1991; DfEE, 1998). There is evidence that it is good practice for a child to develop a close relationship with a 'key person', who provides continuity of care for the child and lessens the separation anxiety for the child/parent relationship (Goldschmied and Jackson, 1993; Penn, 1999). However, there is little evidence or training to suggest how practitioners in the role of key person can best cope with the close relationships they make with the children, and the complexity of the triangular relationship with the child's parent. As acknowledged by Goldschmied and Selleck (1996):

> Powerful feelings that may include jealousy and rivalry will need to be acknowledged and supported in a careful management programme of

support and supervision for the key people. (Goldschmied and Selleck, 1996 p13)

The constant debate about attachment has long led many staff in nurseries to shy away from close attachments with children, fearing that the parent will be unable to cope. Evidence suggests that parents who choose nursery childcare in preference to childminders or nannies, do so because they fear the child will form a close attachment to an individual carer, ostracising the parent and exacerbating their feelings of guilt about returning to work. It could be argued that there are too many reasons not to implement a key person system in a nursery, if it leads to anxiety for parents and for the practitioner (Goldschmied and Jackson, 1993). Elfer, Goldschmied and Selleck (2003) would argue to the contrary, claiming that the benefits to the child are overwhelming. Moreover, they suggest that the complex relationship difficulties surrounding a key person approach are 'challenges to be overcome, rather than reasons *not* to develop the key person approach' (p12).

The role of the adult cannot be over-emphasised in the caring and educating of young children. Research suggests that adults who are really in tune with the child will be able to support the child much more successfully than the adult who is not. Bion (1962) considers the concept of 'containment' as the adult noticing the child's distress, understanding it and thereby responding to the child's emotional needs. The child then feels looked after and emotionally contained. The practicalities of caring for babies and young children cannot be dealt with in isolation as it is the very essence of the relationship that makes it challenging. It is the physical cuddling, handling and holding of babies that essentially forms the close bonds with the key person, as described by Goldschmied and Selleck (1996),

> Through intimate and tender patterns of body play, gestures and conversations with their key person children become attuned and responsive to others. (Goldschmied and Selleck, 1996 p6).

By carefully observing children, it is possible to determine their level of well being by considering their level of involvement in an activity. Laevers (1997) suggests a child has a high level of involvement when deeply involved in an activity. Laevers (1997) designed a scale to determine levels of 'well-being' and 'involvement'. By using the scale as a point of reference, it is possible to determine whether the child has a high, medium or low level of involvement.

The rights of young children and their developing relationships with each other

If, as brain studies suggest, the infant is an active participant from birth and the adult is significant to the development of the child, how much do we know about the relationship of the infant with other children? Building on the knowledge that babies are alert to their mothers or significant adults, researchers have employed similar methods to observe children communicating with each other in their first year of life (Goldschmied and Selleck, 1996). The need for stimulation and continuous relationships is demonstrated as young babies interact with each other, playing with the contents of a 'treasure basket'. These baskets contain everyday objects, chosen because of the sensory experiences they offer to babies who can sit up but not yet crawl, thus extending their opportunities for exploration and learning. In the video *Infants at Work* (Goldschmied, 1989), babies can be seen interacting with each other, although it had been thought that infants showed no interest in each other (Goldschmied and Jackson, 1994; Selleck and Griffin, 1996).

Some researchers consider that 'adults have the power to support or 'shut down' or disrupt these friendships' (Whaley and Rubenstein, 1994 p399). If this is true, then the role of the key person is crucial in supporting the children's friendships. Further evidence of very young children developing attachments to others in their key group is illustrated by Selleck and Griffin (1996) and by Goldschmied and Selleck (1996) in their account of babies exchanging looks, touch and vocalisations. This view is also supported by Gopnik, Meltzoff and Kuhl (1999) in their account of the responses of babies to others. If, as new research indicates, babies are responsive to the children with whom they come into close contact on a regular basis, as in group day care, is this early evidence of developing friendships between babies? And if so, what is the significance? After viewing the video clips repeatedly, researchers suggest that these early friendships can impact on the way in which children become future citizens (Goldschmied and Selleck, 1996). Research suggests that 'children are born poised to learn' (Nutbrown, 1996 p102) and that caring and significant adults are vital to children's learning and development.

The 1989 United Nations Convention on the Rights of the Child, adopted by the United Kingdom in 1991, sets out a number of articles relating to the rights of young children and people up to the age of eighteen years. It may be difficult to comprehend how this could be applied to babies. However, parents and practitioners can empower children and respect their rights by creating a respectful environment and by giving them a choice.

A framework of support for practitioners

In the DfES *Framework of Effective Practice* (2002) Professor Lesley Abbott and her team have the *Birth to Three Matters* framework. The project, set up in direct response to a Government Green Paper (DfEE, 2000) was DfES and Sure Start-funded. Practitioners were consulted in order to gain their views about such a framework. Initial concerns about curricula for babies or the development of a watered down version of the Foundation Stage (DfEE, 2000) were allayed. The publication and dissemination of *Birth to Three Matters* (DfES/Sure Start, 2003) has provided practitioners with long overdue support emphasising the need to balance physical care and attention with the development of emotional bonds with babies and young children.

Children under three years of age learn better if they form strong emotional attachments with one or two special people, who are generally understood and determined as their key person in the group setting. There are many complex challenges to the key person approach: practitioners require support and guidance to enable them to manage effective relationships within the triangle of child, parent and practitioner.

Interviewing key academics

The rationale underpinning my research was that working with children under three is an area largely neglected in the 29 targets set by the DfES for the Early Years Development and Childcare Partnerships. However, in the Green Paper (DfEE, 2000) the government's support and promise to develop 'a framework of best practice for supporting children from birth-3' is recognised. (Professor Abbott, who was leading the project, renamed the framework from 'best' practice to 'effective' practice.) I thought that key academics in the field would identify a number of issues about working with under threes. So I planned to interview Lesley Abbott, Tricia David and Peter Elfer. The interviews for this study explore what these academics (professionally and personally) considered the key issues about working with under threes to be.

Interpreting the data

I began each interview by asking: What do you think are the key issues when working with under threes? The coding method I developed in my framework for analysis suggested that there were several themes running through the answers to the first question:

- the need for warm and responsive relationships
- the possibility of misunderstandings about child protection issues, holding, and physical contact
- responsive carers
- understanding of young children
- staff having the ability to de-centre
- trained staff and staff training
- consistency
- quality
- key person approach/multiple attachments

The key issue throughout the interviews was the recurring theme of the relationships babies and children form with the adults and other children in their lives, particularly in a group care situation. How this was expressed differed but sometimes the wording corresponded exactly when talking about the role of the key person:

> An identification of one or two people who are key, who make a strong relationship with the young child. (Lesley Abbott)

> Well I think in working with them, for me the most important thing is the warm and sound responsiveness of the staff. (Tricia David)

> The main issue is relationship. The kind of relationships staff make with the children. (Peter Elfer)

Child protection

Misunderstandings about child protection issues were raised as a concern by all three academics. Their concerns were similar: they felt that staff sometimes misunderstood child protection issues completely so that children were being denied physical attention such as cuddling or holding. Tricia David explained how her work in other European countries always made her see things differently:

> For example, Helen Penn always says that in Britain we are always hung up on child abuse so we are looking for it everywhere and so children's nudity isn't accepted and I think there is a piece in one of her books where she talks about a male worker putting suntan oil on a child, and the children were in the nude and I am not sure if it was Spain or Italy, whichever it was, she said all of a sudden she realised, she too had got this kind of English hang up and she spoke to the head of the centre and they laughed at her. (Tricia David)

> The intimate physical handling of the children by a man preparing them for nude play in the fountain, creaming their bodies vigorously with suntan oil, towelling them down and in settling them to sleep, when

one fidgety girl was hauled on to his lap and held there firmly – is another aspect which as an English observer I find surprising. Such is the concern for child abuse that men touching children in this way would not be allowed in an English nursery. But when I raise this with the administrators, it is regarded as unproblematic, and as an Anglo-American obsession. (Penn, 1997 p86)

Tricia David continued to emphasise the need to be aware of child protection issues but said: 'I am fearful that we are moving too far away from cuddling children, and all this and being very natural with them'. Peter Elfer expressed similar concerns, suggesting that there were a great many misunderstandings with regard to child protection:

Nursery nurses are bombarded with all sorts of very unclear messages about child sexual abuse and are very careful about physical contact. Of course they must be. It is a real issue, it is very important that children are protected in that sense. But there is a risk, if Staff are too inhibited, of a lack of intimacy and contact. (Peter Elfer)

He also informed me of a draft policy that had been written about the restraining and handling of primary and secondary school children with disruptive behaviour, which was completely appropriate in that context. However, the policy had been extended down the whole age range, to not only the three and four year olds but also to the babies. It said things like 'contact will be kept to a minimum', which may be appropriate for some older children but as Peter Elfer suggested, 'almost the opposite is true for a baby, they need a lot of physical contact'. He suggested this was an area of great concern and that it was particularly difficult and anxiety-provoking for an inexperienced nursery worker to receive such a message:

If they pick up a baby or put a baby on their lap somebody is going to turn round and say 'You are not behaving professionally' or even worse somebody is going to say 'You are behaving abusively'. (Peter Elfer)

Trained staff and staff training

Staff training also emerged as a key concern. Lesley Abbott spoke to me about the importance of appropriate training and particularly emphasised the need to include training about the birth to three years age range on teaching courses:

I think it is important that all training, for whatever role, addresses the birth onwards stage, particularly teacher education. Three to five is recognised as an early years specialism in Teacher Education but there is a tendency to ignore the birth to three age range. The Senior Practitioner route and the Foundation degree are concentrating on birth to three modules. The statement of requirement is quite clear in specifying that the birth to three age range must be covered in training. (Lesley Abbott)

Tricia David highlighted the need for staff training but also emphasised the importance of 'helping staff not only understand cognitively that they mature emotionally and socially themselves'. Peter Elfer supported the importance of staff training but also suggested that training needs to be supported by the heads of organisations such as managers, supervisors, and heads of centres. Lesley Abbot advised that practitioners accept research findings and recognise the government views that care and education are inseparable (Abbott and Moylett, 1997 p20). Peter Elfer, however, proposes that in the UK this has yet to be achieved: 'I think we have got this tradition in this country of splitting off care and education, and education has been thought about a lot'. He qualified his statement with regard to practitioners' perceptions of each other's role where there is a range of age groups, such as in a day nursery. This view is endorsed by Lindon (2000), who at first considered that the split was between teachers and nursery nurses but then decided that the split was between staff working with the over threes and those working with the under threes. Peter Elfer continued:

> There is a belief that if you work with very young children it is in-herently less skilled, less demanding, less sophisticated and less im-portant. I suppose it is the kind of rule of thumb that works right throughout the education system, the older the people you work with, the cleverer or more important you are, and it really seems to me almost the reverse – that you need intellectual ability, and emotional intelligence or ability most of all, to work with babies. (Peter Elfer)

The key person

Lesley Abbott describes quality as being of central importance; quality of the provision, resources, staff and the relationships they make with the children. All three respondents held firm views of the importance of a key person system linking practitioners, parents and children in a close relationship. Lesley Abbott sees the key person as providing consistency for the child, particularly at times of intimacy, such as feeding and changing. Her view is that babies need to make 'strong attachments' to one or two people who are key. She suggests that multiple attachments are practical in a group setting where a child may be present for long periods of time during which staff shifts change. Forming a strong relationship with more than one person can help to overcome this organisational element but still enables the child to enjoy close personal relationships.

Tricia David also defines the key person approach as important but she acknowledges that some parents may be anxious about their child making attachments to the key person. She suggests that it is important for staff to understand the feelings of parents and are able to 'de-centre in terms of parents'. She considers that staff should be able to nurture families and take on a 'grandparent' role. Peter Elfer strongly supports the role of the key person approach and celebrates the work of Elinor Goldschmied, Sonia Jackson and Dorothy Selleck. Furthermore, from his own research, he also finds that parents can become concerned about the key person taking over their parental role.

In his book (Elfer, Goldschmied and Selleck, 2003) about the role of the key person in a nursery setting, Peter Elfer states how parents had told him, that they wanted their child(ren) to form relationships with practitioners in the nursery that were close and special 'but not *too special*'. He agrees with Lesley Abbott about 'multiple attachments', acceding that, provided this is limited to only a few people, a 'back up person is so important'. Tricia David suggests that advice and support are very important to practitioners who are key workers but Peter Elfer goes much further. He explains how he was influenced by the work of Menzies-Lyth (1959) on anxiety and staff turnover in a general hospital. He describes how he compared Menzies-Lyth's study to practice in the day nursery setting. From his own research and findings from other disciplines, Elfer states that there is evidence that staff avoid getting too closely involved with the children in their care, for fear of upsetting the parent. He observes that in order to manage their feelings, nursery workers keep incredibly busy. Although there are many practical tasks in a nursery setting that need to be carried out, he suggests that nursery workers either keep busy or 'go into a world of their own' as a defence against getting too involved. He continues:

> The kind of emotional demands on nursery workers haven't been addressed very well and until we get that right, the complaint that nursery nurses don't notice what babies are doing or the view that 'babies are boring' to look after, will continue. (Peter Elfer)

On the need for advisors, Tricia David suggests that the 'single most important thing is a proper supervision system', and Peter Elfer agrees. Support from managers can help practitioners deal with the complexities of the relationships in which they find themselves, particularly those who work in baby rooms. Caring for the educator is an important point made by Selleck and Griffin (1996). They suggest that sensitive supervision and in-service training will help to support practitioners' health and wellbeing.

The role of men

Views about the role of men working with under threes showed over-lapping concerns, particularly with regard to child protection. All the respondents suggested that child protection was not an easy issue for families or indeed for men who are, or would be, practitioners (Cameron, Moss and Owen, 1999). Peter Elfer's comments are based on research that suggests that men are statistically more guilty than women of sexual abuse, although he is certain that men have a place in working with the very young, to provide a more balanced experience for children. Lesley Abbott echoes some of Peter Elfer's concerns, suggesting that society in general has a long way to go before accepting and feeling comfortable with the role of men working with very young children (Jensen, 1996). Tricia David argues as an advocate for men working with the very young, although she is aware of child protection issues. She told me a poignant story about how one of her former male students had spoken out about being mindful of being accused of potential abuse, and how by being 'aware', it was possible to deal with it.

Did they think a 'witnessing policy', such as a female member of staff witnessing other male and female staff during intimate care routines, would help to overcome fears of child abuse? Tricia David said that if it made people feel better and provided it was applied to either gender, it might be useful. But the other two do not believe that witnessing policies are enough. More important is for practitioners to have the time, support and opportunity to reflect on their practice. 'Child protection is one of those issues they need time to talk about and air their concerns in a group where they won't feel threatened' (Lesley Abbott). 'It is absolutely essential that regular time is set aside for staff to talk about their inter-actions together and their interactions with the children' (Peter Elfer).

All expressed their discomfort about the pay and conditions associated with working in early years and doubted whether more men would be attracted into the field until this was addressed. This view is supported by Scott, Brown and Campbell (1999). They were all particularly keen to emphasise that this did not mean that low pay was acceptable to women. Lesley Abbott referred to Denmark, where the pedagogues (many of whom are male) have a high status and role, childcare being a high status activity in Scandinavia generally (Cameron, Moss and Owen, 1999).

Key policies

Which key policies did they consider had influenced under threes pro-vision? Tricia David suggests that women had been actively discouraged from working until the new Labour government came into office. Although she celebrates some of their policies such as increasing the quantity and the quality of provision for children's learning, she fears that their targets were more about raising achievements in literacy and numeracy than about holistic learning. She thinks informal care had been neglected and recalled the experiences of her own daughters who had both employed nannies to care for their children in their own homes. The arrangement had been very successful, particularly as both the nannies were part of a good support network. This prompted her to wonder what support was available for informal care arrangements where there was no established support mechanism. This echoed Peter Elfer's view that support for practitioners is essential.

Lesley Abbott also believes that Labour has been instrumental with regard to childcare policy. She cites the National Childcare Strategy (DfEE, 1998), the Early Years Development and Childcare Partnerships (DfEE, 1998) and the 'real effort' made in practical terms by the DfES in setting up a special unit for Early Years. Lesley Abbott says she was encouraged by the expansion of the Early Excellence Centres (DfEE, 1997) and the Sure Start early intervention programme (DfEE, 1998), and the links between health and education for the most disadvantaged families. Peter Elfer, on the other hand, argues that the operational budgets in Early Excellence Centres and their allocation of resources and space to release staff compares favourably to the private nurseries, which have no such capacity. He criticises the market economy, suggesting that if teachers were paid on the fees that parents could afford, the education system would be in the same poor condition as the system in place for the youngest children in the country. He adds that low status, coupled with low pay and a lack of opportunity or time for discussion with the manager, makes it difficult for practitioners to feel recognised and acknowledged.

With reference to government policy, Lesley Abbott says:

> In choosing to look at Early Years as one of their particular focuses the House of Commons Select Committee on Education actively took evidence from people who were working with the very young. This helped to raise the status of young children in the eyes of Ministers and M.Ps. Ministers like Margaret Hodge and Baroness Ashton who have a particular responsibility for young children have done much to ensure that early years is high on the political agenda. The fact that they have responsibility for young children means that there is somebody 'fighting their corner' and supporting the issue of 'joined up thinking' and multidisciplinary work. (Lesley Abbott)

She also says that the Foundation Stage (DfEE, 2000) together with the Green Paper (DfEE 2000) had recognised the need to:

Safeguard the birth to three stage. The DfES project to develop a Framework to support practitioners working with children from birth to three
was an important way of giving national recognition to the birth to
three age group. It is certainly not going to be seen as a National Curriculum for the under threes. (Lesley Abbott)

She welcomes the practical guide for professionals working with disabled children, *Together from the Start* (DfES, 2002), which aims to support families with children from birth to two years, 'It is encouraging
that guidelines are being produced which highlight the importance of
babies and very young children.'

Key research studies
Because the three informants are academics and their views are informed by research, I asked them to identify key research studies which
had influenced their thinking. Lesley Abbott cited the wealth of research
in neuroscience as being highly significant, supporting the idea that children are already pre-programmed to learn (Trevarthen, 1992). She
quotes several scientists who have carried out research on brain studies:
Greenough, Greenspan, Greenfield, Colwyn, Trevarthen and John Bruer,
as well as the popular studies by Gopnik, Meltzoff and Kuhl (1999).
Lesley Abbott emphasises Goldschmied and Jackson's (1994) development of the 'Treasure Basket' and 'Heuristic Play' which highlight the
importance of providing opportunities for babies and toddlers to explore
everyday objects, closely observed by adults, but without their intervention. Gardner's work on multiple intelligence has been significant in
identifying different kinds of intelligence (Gardner, 1983). The research
on emotional literacy (Hoy, 1998; Tobias, 2000) and Goldman's recognition of the significance of the emotional quotient (EQ), as opposed to
overemphasis on the IQ, has been an important breakthrough. Peter Elfer
speaks of the importance of brain studies and pre-natal developments, a
view endorsed by Tricia David when she says she wished the information
could be harnessed to encourage parents to stimulate their babies from
an early age. In her example she describes a scene in an airport lounge,
where babies in buggies were ignored instead of being included in conversations. She again links this back to her own childhood experiences
and the fact that she had been 'included' from an early age:

I can still picture.. I can still be the little one sitting on the rug by my
Nan's range, she had an old kitchen range then, behind me and watching everybody talking. It's like, you know here's the room and I'm here
and they're all round, so I was very much... even if I couldn't be part of
the conversation in terms of saying things. They used to have political
rows – it was wonderful – but I was still part, I wasn't pushed to one side
of it. (Tricia David)

Tricia David compares England unfavourably with other European countries, where young children are welcome in restaurants and made to feel special. She says that her return to England was a shock, when she realised that English people were astonished and confused if they saw an adult absorbed in speaking to their baby. She is 'excited by new research ideas' and says she had been privileged to work with Corinne Hutt in the 1970s, which had endorsed her 'love of reading research studies.' However, she considers it was her own childhood and mothering experiences which most influenced her thinking. She recalls being raised by her grandmother because her mother had gone out to work during the war, and that she had 'the most wonderful childhood'. Her idea that children needed to be with lots of people, not just their mothers, had come directly from her own experience.

Horrified by Bowlby, she was pleased to discover Rutter (1972). She likens her own upbringing to a mini-version of being raised in a compound, where children form multiple attachments as the norm. She feels that while she had found studies such as those by Rutter and later brain studies such as Gopnik, Meltzoff and Kuhl (1999) interesting and 'beautifully written,' they also confirm what she has always felt. Peter Elfer argues that attachment theory is an important area of research but that it is more in line with psychoanalytical concepts of containment and transference and that Bowlby's work 'has been so much used against women that there is a kind of instinctive hostility towards it'.

Raising her family of two young daughters in France, Tricia David understands the stress of the responsibility of caring for children and the need to share it. Also confirming her own views was the television programme about gorillas (Fossey, 1983) showing how the baby gorillas were passed around so that the mother did not have sole care. She says: 'I think if we lived in groups, that's what would happen.' She goes on to recount a story of a young friend whose baby had died – a 'cot-death'. The police would not allow the mother to touch the body. She says: 'I can remember as a young mum thinking my God, I'd just want to hold them and hold them'. The programme about the gorillas had shown a baby gorilla that had died being carried around by the mother for about three days. 'By the third day she has accepted that the baby is dead; and I thought: we don't know how to do it, we just don't know how to do it'. It is important to recognise that 'we are animals' but 'we do not seem to accept what our bodies need'. Her association with Fossey's theories about primates (1983) provided a fascinating perspective.

The role of parents

All three agreed that parents were children's first educators. They all spoke about the role of parents with practitioners and the need for sensitivity when the child makes attachments to key people in the nursery or childcare situation. Lesley Abbott says that the home link was crucial in the life and 'out of home' context of the child, a view endorsed by Penn (1999). Peter Elfer and Tricia David suggest that parents often feel unable to ask for specific details about their child's day for fear that the practitioner feels that they did not trust them with the care of their child.

Peter Elfer emphasises the importance of the key person building the triangular relationship with the parent and the child, and the need for the manager to support this relationship. Tricia David suggested that the practitioner was ideally placed to share in the 'love' of the child and Lesley Abbott echoes this, suggesting that technology could play a part in 'sharing in a child's first steps'. Photographing children's first moments meant far more than the routine exchange of information about how much food the child had eaten that day. All felt that it was equally important for parents to understand and respect the role of the practitioner.

The impact of current policy development

Peter Elfer is frustrated at having a Foundation Stage that starts at three and Tricia David feels confident that *Birth to Three Matters* (DfES/Sure Start, 2003) will re-affirm the practice of many effective practitioners and help those who are less confident. She wants more recognition for practitioners who work with the youngest children and is concerned about the lack of research into why some people don't talk to their babies. Lesley Abbott stresses the importance of international studies and the move toward a focus on under threes in Masters degree programmes.

Conclusion: topics for future research

The most cogent message from the three interviews was the importance of the relationships that babies and young children forge with the adults who care for them. Staffing was a key theme for all concerned and I agree with Lesley Abbott:

> I would fight to the death the view that anybody can look after and work with young children. They deserve the finest minds and the best trained people to be responsible for their care and education.

It is difficult to summarise interviews so rich in content, but some key emphases emerged. Lesley Abbott speaks about the importance of *policy change and the effectiveness of the present Government policy.* Tricia David considers research studies to be extremely important but suggests that *her own experiences as a child and as a mother* mattered as much and were a fundamental influence. Peter Elfer, after observing many children and staff in numerous nursery settings, comes to the conclusion that *relationships were only as effective as the managers who supported them.*

New theories are proposed by Tricia David and Peter Elfer that require further research. Tricia David's anxiety about parents not including children in conversation suggests an opportunity for further investigation. If, as she suggests, some parents do not feel comfortable speaking to their babies in public, does it suggest they do not speak to their babies at home? It would be interesting to consider further studies on the effects of communal living and of primates' care of their young.

The most challenging hypothesis was the influence of psychoanalytical and psychological theory and the work of Isabel Menzies-Lyth (1959), identified by Peter Elfer. The early evidence from his own research suggests that practitioners in the role of key person require extensive support from their managers to facilitate the complex triangular relationship that exists between child, parent and carer.

The three leading academics in this study identified many issues when working with babies and children under three, and in particular that:

■ *relationships* between adults and children in their care is vital.

■ highly skilled, motivated and sensitive practitioners are required for the care of young children.

■ the *key person* caring for babies and young children needs strong emotional support to sustain a complex and rewarding relationship with both the child(ren) and the parents.

The views of Selleck and Griffin (1996) express my own view of how it might be for our youngest children:

> We must have the courage to insist on the best, not just an adequate quality of education and care with 'fit persons' for babies and toddlers. We need the vision to plan for whole human beings who have a clear and realistic personal identity whatever combination of cultural or religious background, racial origins, gender, ability or disability that may be. Children who know who they are will have the confidence to love and learn and communicate in a world of mathematical, scientific, aesthetic and technological experiences. Children who can collaborate and learn together in harmony with other people are likely to respect and value differences. Children who are able to have intimate respon-

sive relationships with their significant adult will have better access to relevant learning experiences. Children who play in inspirational, safe and challenging environments will take these values into adulthood and pass them onto future generations. An ethos of respect and dignity in childhood may be set from the cradle to the grave. (Selleck and Griffin, 1996 p169)

References

Abbott, L. and Moylett, H. (1997) *Working with the Under-3s: responding to children's needs*, Bristol: Open University Press

Bion, W. (1962) *Learning from Experience*, London, Heinemann

Blaxter, L. Hughes, C. and Tight, M. (2001) *How to Research: second edition*, Buckingham: Open University Press

Bowlby, J. (1965) (2nd edition) *Child care and the Growth of Love.* Middlesex: Penguin Books

Bowlby, J. (1984) 2nd edition *Attachment and loss: Volume 1 Attachment,* London: Penguin Books.

Brierley, J. (1994) (2nd edition) *Give me a child until he is seven: Brain Studies and Early Childhood Education*, London, The Falmer Press

Cameron, C. Moss, P. and Owen, C. (1999) *Men in the Nursery: gender and caring work.* London: Paul Chapman

David, T. (1999) Valuing Young Children in Abbott, L and Moylett, H (eds) (1999) *Early Education Transformed*, London: Falmer Press

Department for Education and Employment (1999) *New qualifications framework: A Newsletter for the Early years Development and Childcare Partnerships*, partners 5, September 1999, London: DfEE

Department for Education and Employment (1990) *Starting with Quality: Report of the Committee of Inquiry into the Educational Experiences Offered to 3 and 4 Year Olds.* London:HMSO

Department for Education and Employment (1998) *Meeting the Childcare Challenge: a framework and consultation document.* London: DfEE

Department for Education and Employment (2000) *Curriculum Guidance for the Foundation Stage* London: DfEE/Qualifications and Curriculum Authority

Department for Education and Employment (2000) *Select Committee on Education and Employment* London: DfEE

Department for Education and Employment, (1996) *Nursery and Grant Maintained Schools Act* London: HMSO

Department for Education and Employment, (1997) *Excellence in Schools*, White Paper, London: DfEE

Department for Education and Skills (2002) *Together from the Start*, London: DfES

Department for Education and Skills/Sure Start (2002) *Framework of Effective Practice. Consultation document.* London: DfES/ Sure Start

Department for Education and Skills, (2001) *National Standards for Under Eights Day Care and Childminding: Full Day Care*, Nottingham: HMSO

Department for Education and Skills and Sure Start (2003) *Birth to three matters:a framework to support children in their earliest years of life.* Nottingham: HMSO

Department of Health, (1991) *The Children Act 1989, Guidance and Regulations, Volume 2, Family Support, Day Care and Educational Provision for Young Children.* London: HMSO

Department of Science (1948) *Nursery and Childminding Regulation Act.* London: HMSO

Elfer, P. Goldschmied, E. and Selleck, D. (2003) *Key Persons in Nurseries: Building relationships for quality provision,* London: Early Years Network

Fossey, D. (1983) *Gorillas in the Mist,* Boston, Hougham: Miffin

Gardner, H. (1983) *Frames of mind: The theory of multiple intelligences,* Harvard: Harvard University Press

Glass, N. (1999) 'Sure Start: The Development of an Early Intervention Programme for Young Children in the United Kingdom', *Children and Society* Volume 13 (1999), pp.257-264 London: John Wiley and Sons

Goldschmied, E and Jackson, S. (1994) *People Under Three: Young Children in Day Care.* London: Routledge

Goldschmied, E. and Selleck, D. (1996) *Communication between babies in their first year,* London: National, Children's Bureau.

Gopnik, A., Meltzoff, A. and Kuhl, P. (1999) *How babies think.* London: Weindenfield and Nicholson

Hennessy, E, Martin, S, Moss, P and Melhuish E (1992) *Children and Day Care; Lessons from Research,* London, Paul Chapman Publishing

HMSO (1988) *Education Reform Act:40* London: HMSO

Hoy, G. (1998) *Multiple Intelligences and Emotional Literacy:* ONLINE

Jensen, J.J. (1996) *Men as Workers in Childcare Services: A discussion paper.* European Commission Network on Childcare and other measures to reconcile Employment and Family Responsibilities for Women and Men. Brussels: European Equal opportunities Unit.

Laevers, F. (1997) *A Process-Orientated Child Follow-up System for Young Children,* Leuven: Centre for Experiential Education.

Lindon, J (2000) *Helping babies and toddlers learn : a guide to good practice with under-threes,* London, National Early Years Network

Menzies Lyth, I. (1959) The functioning of social systems as a defence against anxiety: a report on the study of the nursing service of a general hospital, *Human Relations* 13:95-121

Menzies Lyth, I (1988) *Containing anxiety in institutions; Selected essays: Volume 1* London: Free Association Books

Moss, P. and Melhuish, E. (1991) *Current Issues in day care for Young children,* London: HMSO

Nutbrown, C. (1996) *Respectful Educators – Capable Learners Children's Rights and Early Education,* London, Paul Chapman Publishing

Ofsted, (2001) *Full Day Care: Guidance to the National Standards,* London: HMI

Penn, H. (1997) *Comparing Nurseries: Staff and Children in Italy, Spain and the UK* London: Paul Chapman

Penn, H (1999) How should we care for babies and toddlers? An analysis of practice in out-of-home settings for children under three, *Childcare Resource and Research Unit,* University of Toronto Canada, Occasional paper 10.6.1999 iv, 66pp

Rutter, M. (1972) *Maternal Deprivation Reassessed,* Middlesex, Penguin Books

Scott, G., Brown, U. and Campbell, J. (1999) *Visible Childcare: Invisible Workers, Research Findings No3,* Glasgow: Scottish Poverty Unit

Selleck, D. and Griffin, S. (1996) Quality For The Under Threes in Pugh, G (1996) (ed) (2nd edition) *Contemporary issues in the Early Years: Working Collaboratively for Children*, London, Paul Chapman

Tobias, S (2000) '*The Feelings of Vocabulary' The Children's Emotional Literacy Project* ONLINE:<http://www.kidseq.com/articles.html> Last updated 26th September 2000 (accessed 23rd August 2002)

Trevarthen, C (1992) An infants motives for speaking and thinking in the culture, in David, T, (1999) *Valuing Young Children* in Abbott, L and Moylett, H (eds) (1999) *Early Education Transformed*, London, Falmer Press

Whaley, K. L. and Rubenstein, T. S. (1994) How Toddlers 'do' Friendship: a descriptive analysis of naturally occurring friendships in a group child care setting, *Journal of social and personal Relationships*, 11,3 pp.383-400

11

Using young children's drawings for teaching and learning: a case study

Karen Boardman

This chapter sprang from an interest in Athey's (1990) work on a five-year Early Education Project carried out at the Froebel Institute in London and Nutbrown's (1999) detailed observations of children aged three to five years in *Threads of Thinking*. Supporting and developing children's thinking through positive interpretations of children's behaviour are key themes throughout both these projects. This, along with information gathered from Reggio Emilia, fuelled my wish to extend my own interest in children's drawings.

As an early years educator and parent, I have always been enthusiastic about children's drawings and mark-makings. But I often wondered what value children place on their drawings. What motivates nursery-aged children to draw imaginatively or representatively? Do children need adult intervention when drawing? Why do some children enjoy drawing and others require coaxing to be enthusiastic about it? What happens to the drawings when it is time to change the display? What value do early educators place on children's drawings? What value do parents/carers place on their children's drawings?

Aim of the study

The study reported here explores how young children's drawings are used by teachers, parents/carers and children in a village nursery class. Over a seven month period the following questions were addressed:

■ How are children's drawings used in teaching and learning?

■ What value do children place on their drawings?

■ How do early educators, parents and carers perceive the value of children's drawings?

This study takes the form of a case study, with direct unstructured observation notes, children's drawings/representations, photographs and a questionnaire as sources of data. A fellow nursery teacher commented on the emerging findings.

Context

Twelve children (seven boys and five girls) aged between three and five participated in this study. They all attended a nursery class in a small village school and all previously attended the school's under twos provision, either full or part time. The nursery class includes white European, Chinese, Italian and Asian children. Ten of the twelve attended nursery full time, the others mornings only.

The classroom is typical of a traditional nursery school, containing a wide range of materials set out in identifiable areas. Children are free to choose between tabletop and carpet activities. They have access to all the resources and materials, which are clearly labelled and freely accessible. The mark-making area is well resourced and available throughout the day. Group activities such as stories, circle time, rhymes and singing, are led by the nursery teacher and the nursery nurse. The key informants of this case study are the twelve children, the nursery nurse and myself, the nursery teacher.

Ethics

Careful consideration was given to the ethical issues of informed consent, confidentiality, protection of informants and the ownership of data, Sieber (1993). Organisational consent was given priority, as I wanted to carry out research within the daily activities of my role in the nursery classroom.

I gained permission from the headteacher and after meeting all the parents, they agreed to involvement in the study. I introduced the study informally to staff and gained their agreement to respond to a questionnaire. Both my teaching and nursery nurse colleagues agreed to read my field notes and observations and make comments. I talked informally to the children about the project at circle time, and towards the end of the research I discussed their drawings with them. I felt it important for them to have their say.

Marsh (2001 p4) suggests that if children are not at the stage where they can be fully informed about the research process, then they cannot 'logically give their consent'. However, I believed that had the children not been interested they would simply have chosen to do something else! I anticipated that children's interest in the project would vary at different times during the seven months of observations and was careful to respect this.

> Children should be told as much as possible, even if some of them cannot understand the full explanation. Their age should not diminish their rights, although their level of understanding must be taken into account in the explanations that are shared with them. (Fine and Sandstrom, 1988 p88)

Thompson (1992 p60) suggests that 'depending on the context and the complexity of the judgement, children at most ages are capable of making decisions concerning what they want to do'. Morrow and Richards (1996 p94) suggest that 'discussions of children's competence to consent usually focus on the age of the children concerned'. Tymchuk (1992 p128) refers to informed consent as happening when someone 'voluntarily agrees to participate in a research project, based on a full disclosure of pertinent information'. Weithorn and Steiner (1994) and Marsh (2001) advocate the importance of involving children in the process of making decisions about taking part in a research project at the design stage. Respect of children's rights to be consulted and involved (or not, depending on their wishes) should be a reflective and responsive process, open to review and analysis. Thomas and O'Kane (1998) ensured their work remained open to children's understanding within their project by arranging group meetings to ask and answer questions relevant to the children's own concerns, using participatory research techniques giving children control over the process and finally by sharing ideas and views with the children through a series of 'activity days'.

The children were always asked if it would be 'okay to do some writing when I am watching you draw/play?', as I have always done for any observation purposes. It is unfortunate if they say 'no', but it happens!

All names of the children, staff, parents and carers have been changed to ensure anonymity and where possible they are referred to by their group (e.g. parent). Confidentiality and anonymity remain major ethical concerns throughout this case study; nevertheless I am confident that process and outcomes caused no harm to the participants.

Method

Direct observation is a reliable and useful way to discover what is actually happening in a setting (Nisbet and Watt, 1980 p13), and unstructured observations with a specific focus were my main source of data.

It was the intention of this study to be specifically concerned with 'how?' within the classroom socio-culture and to enhance my own awareness of how children's drawings are used in teaching and learning. Merriam (1988 p23) refers to ethnographic case studies as 'more than an intensive, holistic description and analysis of a social unit or phenomenon. It is a socio-cultural analysis of the unit of study. Concern with the cultural context is what sets this type of study apart.' I am devoting time by looking in detail at something to which I have not previously paid much attention. Clough and Nutbrown (2002) could well describe this as 'making the familiar strange', as Garfinkel (1967) infers, by paying extraordinary attention to the most commonplace activities, we may learn about them as phenomena in their own right. The purpose of this particular study is to find something out; to focus on children's drawings and look closely at how they are used within the context of my own nursery classroom.

Children's drawings can be valuable data (Goodnow, 1977; Marsh, 2001). The drawings collected in this study were used to support my observations and field notes.

How the children used drawing for their own learning

The children in this study used drawing for varied purposes:

■ to further develop their understanding

■ to investigate a new concept

■ to extend their fun

■ to represent an idea

■ to explain or recall their new and existing experiences

■ to commemorate an interesting happening

■ to offer as a gift

Several interpretations could be suggested for the children's learning as they draw, as the following extracts of observations show.

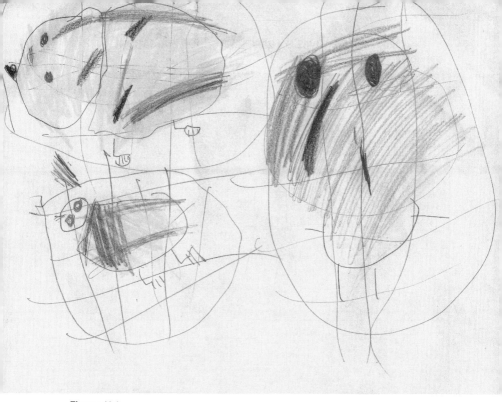

Figure 11.1

The chicks

One of the parents had brought to the nursery some newly hatched chicks from their farm. There were nine three day old chicks in a cardboard box. The children were able to stroke and hold the chicks, and asked lots of questions. Afterwards we looked at picture books about chicks and farms and read a story about a chick.

After lunch the mark-making area was very busy as the children drew pictures of the chicks. I sat and observed some of the children. Madeleine [3:11] (Figure 11.1) drew a picture of three chicks. Carefully she coloured two of them in yellow and put patches of grey on them [the chicks were yellow with patches of grey]. The last chick she coloured grey and purple with great big black eyes. She then circled each chick with an outline and drew lines downwards and across, creating a caged effect. 'They don't like being in a cage. This one here [pointing to the purple and grey chick] has bumped into the fence and it is bruised so it won't lay any more eggs'. Matthew [4:4] (Figure 11.2) looked at Madeleine's drawing and smiled, saying 'they're not in a cage, it's a box'. Matthew had drawn a circle for the chick's head, put eyes and a smiley mouth on his face, then drew two long 'stick' legs and attached two arms to its legs. He then drew a body (I think) starting from one of the legs,

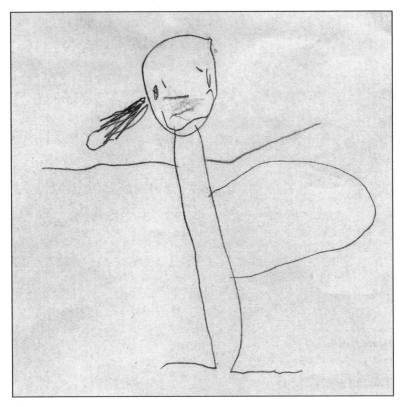

Figure 11.2

making a 'u' shape, ending up back at the same leg. Madeleine put her pencil crayon down and looked at Matthew very crossly, standing with her hands on her hips, replying 'My mummy said that chickens live in pens and that's a cage you know!' Matthew stopped drawing, looked at Madeleine and shouted 'Oh well that's rotten – they will have nowhere to sleep' , to which Madeleine shouted back 'Well my mummy said!' Suzy [4:6] came over to the table to see what all the noise was about. Matthew told Suzy about chicks living in a cage. (Suzy lived on a farm. It was her father who had brought the chicks to the nursey.) Indignantly Suzy spluttered 'It doesn't matter anyway because the snakes are going to eat them!' and went on her way. Matthew picked up his pencil and scribbled next to his chick's eyes. I asked him what he was drawing. 'Well it's crying now because it doesn't like snakes!' he responded, putting his pencil down. (Suzy was correct the chicks would be fed to snakes – but her daddy had told her she must not tell any of the children!) More chicks were drawn that day – all appearing unhappy!

Many and varied interpretations could be discussed within these examples. The learning for the children here could be morally or environmentally centred. Madeleine experimented with her drawing, using colours to make her chick appear bruised and unhappy. Perhaps she had seen chicks cooped up in a cage or perhaps she could sense that the chicks might not like having to live in a cage. Matthew enjoyed drawing his chicks in their box, until he discovered the possibility of their being snake fodder!

Other representations of the chicks drawn on the same day somehow seem to have escaped the feeling of dread for the plight of the chicks.

How I used drawing as an activity to support children's learning

I used drawing for two main purposes: as an activity to introduce a new topic, or to assess a particular learning objective and make class books to develop the children's existing learning. I also used observational drawing as an activity to draw such things as spiders, snails, worms and flowers, as the journal extracts show:

> 'asked the children to draw something beginning with c for our alphabet book'

> 'the children drew pictures of themselves, using mirrors so that they could look carefully, for our topic ourselves – displayed on poster board outside room for parents evening'

> 'working on the colour theme – children drew animals that are black and white'

> 'asked children to draw a picture of their favourite animal after our visit to the zoo – making a book, 'Our Visit to the Zoo', and display board'

Many of the children's drawings were displayed with their permission, on poster boards: 'Elmer', 'Our favourite Pattern', 'Colours', 'Animals', and 'A visit to...', to name but a few. Some drawings were put on the washing line display 'Our Best Work', but mostly the drawings were used to make books, linked to topics, letters, visits and so on. I noticed the children took a large amount of mark-making home at the end of the day.

How the parents used their children's drawings

A questionnaire was sent out to every parent/carer involved in the study, with a covering letter. All of them responded to questions about provision of drawing materials, their ideas on the value of children's drawings and how they themselves used children's drawings.

Provision of materials

Of the twelve parents, seven reported that mark-making materials were readily available at home. Three said that they offered mark-making materials at times as an activity at home, and one said that her child always asked for a pen and paper if he wanted one. Another was reported to do drawing 'at gran's'.

The value of children's drawings

Four out of twelve parents or carers required clarification for this question. The responses showed that they valued drawing for different reasons.

Eight parents felt that drawing supported the development of early writing skills, including how to form letters, and seven specifically mentioned drawing as a way of helping children to learn 'how to hold their pencil correctly'; six parents said that drawing helped children to develop concentration skills and four mentioned 'having new ideas' and using drawing as an 'expression of feeling'.

What do parents do with their children's drawings?

All displayed their children's work in some way: in the bedroom, the study, the kitchen or the car. Five parents said they took drawings to their workplace to display. Ten parents said that they often gave some of their children's drawings to family members, such as the children's gran and auntie. Others talked about using drawings to find out more about their children; one said that she talked to her child about her day and what she had drawn; seven said that they put drawings in a scrapbook to keep them safe. One parent added that she used them to see where her child is 'up to – which stage of development' and another that she 'sorted' them out every so often.

How did early years educators use children's drawings?

Parents' reports of their uses of children's drawings were interesting, but did they differ from those of early childhood educators? A similar questionnaire was used to find out how other teachers and nursery nurses working within the foundation stage in the setting used children's drawings. Four teachers and two nursery nurses agreed to complete the questionnaire.

In all classes in the foundation stage, mark-making materials are provided on a daily basis and accessible at various free-play times.

All six practitioners said they used drawings for display and as part of the work on a theme or topic. Five said that they encouraged drawing after a visit or interesting event, and five specifically mentioned use of drawing to develop language skills.

Practitioners used display much as the parents did but are more pro-active in initiating drawing with children. Interestingly, parents reported keeping, cataloguing or sorting children's drawings, not a practice mentioned by practitioners.

Conclusion

This chapter has provided a glimpse into the fascinating world of children's drawings. Further research is needed to understand more of how practitioners use such representations to support young children's learning.

References

Athey, C. (1990) *Extending Thought in Young Children*. London: Paul Chapman

Clough, P. and Nutbrown, C. (2002) *A Student's Guide to Methodology: Justifying Enquiry*. London: Sage

Fine, G.A. and Sanstrom, K.L. (1998) *Knowing Children: Participant Observation with Minors, Qualitative Research Methods, Series 15* Beverly Hills: Sage

Garfinkel, H. (1967) *Studies in Ethnomethodology*. New Jersey: Prentice Hall

Goodnow, J. (1977) *Children's Drawing*, London: Fontana/Open Books

Marsh, J. (2001) Participatory Research with Young Children, Module 4, Unit 7, pp. 1-21, *Research Methods in Early Childhood Education* Sheffield: Sheffield University Division of Education Press

Merriam, S.B. (1988) *Case Study Research in Education*. San Francisco: Jossey Bass

Morrow, V. and Richards, M. (1996) The Ethics of Social Research with children: An overview. *Children and Society* Vol 10 p90-105

Nisbett, J.D. and Watt, J. (1980) Case Study. *Rediguide* 26, Nottingham: University of Nottingham, School of Education

Nutbrown, C. (1999) *Threads of thinking.* London: Paul Chapman

Plummer, K. (1983) *Documents of Life.* London: Allen and Unwin

Sieber, J. (1993) The Ethics and Politics of Sensitive Research in Rensetti, C. and Lee, R.M. (eds) *Researching Sensitive Topics*. London: Sage

Thomas, N. and O'Kane, C. (1998) *Children and Decision Making: A Summary Report* Swansea: University of Wales

Thompson, R.A. (1992) Developmental Changes in Research, Risk and Benefit. A Changing Calculus of Concerns in Stanley, B. and Sieber, J.E. (eds) *Social Research on Children and Adolescents: Ethical Issues* London: Sage

Tymchuck, A.J. (1992) Assent Processes in Stanley, B. and Sieber, J.E. (eds) *Social Research on Children and Adolescents: Ethical Issues.* London: Sage

Weithorn, L.A. and Steiner, D.G. (1994) Children's Involvement in Research Participation Decisions: Psychological Considerations in Grodin, M. A. and Glantz, L.H. (eds) *Children as Research Subjects: Science Ethics and Law*. Oxford: Oxford University Press

Wellington, J.J. (1996) *Methods and Issues in Educational Research*. Sheffield: University of Sheffield Department of Education

12

Young children's favourite books

Karen Wilkinson

Overview

This chapter explores the reading choices of four pre-school children, their 'favourite' books and the impact of the parents' own reading choices. Parents were interviewed at home, the children's book collections were listed and photographed and parents kept a diary of the books read with their child over a seven day period. All four children had access to a wide range of books, which had been purposefully chosen, with each child's interests and preferences in mind. Whilst parents' childhood memories of books may impact upon some children's choices, parents frame their choices in the context of children's chosen reading. The status of 'favourite' books was defined by the personal meaning it had for each child as displayed by their idiosyncratic and emotional response. Many of the favourite books were not part of the established canon of children's literature.

This chapter describes the research themes, the methodological approach used and presents findings and conclusions.

Children's reading choices

There is little disagreement among researchers about the value of parents reading and re-reading books to foster children's intellectual, social and literacy development. However, so far, research has largely focused on the *how* and *why* of reading familiar books with pre-school children. By comparison we know little about *what* pre-school children are reading and re-reading with their parents, and *why*.

There has long been a debate between those who believe that parents should read only 'quality books' to their pre-school children and those who believe that they should read anything, as long as they read. This debate, as Millard (1997) pointed out, is based on assumptions which completely disregard the value to an individual of a particular book.

In 1977, Elaine Moss wrote about the most important book in her daughter Alison's early life. It was 'a cheap book in every sense of the word' (Moss, 1977 p140) and despite having an array of 'classic' picture-books to choose from, *Peppermint* was the one Alison clamoured for. It was 'never scribbled on, thrown out of bed, lent to a friend or given away with the jumble'(*ibid*, p140). The story of an unwanted kitten who finds a loving home and lives happily ever after was nothing special, except to Alison, who was an adopted child and, like Peppermint, was taken home 'to be loved and cared for and treasured' (*ibid*, p141). Moss concluded:

> The artistically worthless book – hack-written and poorly illustrated – may, if its emotional content is sound, hold a message of supreme significance for a particular child ... For a book by itself is nothing...one can only assess its value by the light it brings to a child's eye. (*ibid*, p142)

Watson reminds us that 'good books have no hallmark – and, if they had one, children would probably disregard it' (Watson, 1992 p1). For a book a child repeatedly goes back to, 'is a book that is speaking to that child' (Waterland, 1985 p42), perhaps reflecting a deep cognitive preoccupation (Holdaway, 1979) or meeting an undiagnosed need (Butler, 1995). Whilst some choices are not always understandable, 'anything as intense as this devotion has to be seen as important' (Butler, 1995 p113). Children read for pleasure (Bettelheim and Zelan, 1982). Interest, surprise, joy and fear are just as much a part of their experience as it is ours (Gopnik *et al*, 2000). And while few would question the assertion that 'much of the decision-making about what children read is done by adults' (Agnew, 1996 p35), young children are not entirely powerless, as demonstrated in Dorothy White's (1954) account of the failure of a Caldecott medal winner: her daughter Carol simply closed the book and walked away.

There is a small bank of studies spanning nearly fifty years conducted by researchers who have turned to their own children (Bissex, 1980; Crago and Crago, 1983; Baghban, 1984; Jones, 1996) or their grandchildren (Campbell, 1999), or to other people's children (Taylor and Strickland, 1986; Minns, 1997; Nutbrown, 2000) to understand how early literacy develops. Librarians have documented their children's (White, 1954) and grandchildren's (Butler, 1979) encounters with books in the same way.

There are only glimpses of information about why these choices were made by these adults: books which were not 'too difficult' (Minns, 1997 p25); a child's interest in numbers (Bissex, 1980); books which recalled family holidays (Wolf and Heath, 1998); books with which to 'indulge the pleasure of our own hearts' (White, 1954 p20); and childhood favourites (Nutbrown, 2000). These studies reveal just how difficult it is for the outsider to distinguish between books children are simply familiar with and those which are favourites. In *Cushla and Her Books,* Cushla's responses exemplify the difference between those books which Cushla liked but was 'not bowled over' by (Butler, 1979 p51) and those for which she had a 'strong attachment' (*ibid*, p27) or were 'superior in impact' (*ibid*, p28). The difference between familiar and favourite is one of intensity and is clearly recognised by those closest to young children. Whitehead (1999) described parents and grandparents as 'powerful insiders'.

Some of the studies describe the physicality of favourite choices: the banging, chewing, kissing, licking, clasping, and carrying. Parents describe the annoying and yet paradoxical pleasure of repeating favourite books (Minns, 1997; Taylor and Strickland, 1986) and the physical pleasure these children find in favourite books (Butler, 1979; Nutbrown, 2000). We see children as young as twelve months old making definite book selections (Campbell, 1999) or even topics within books (Jones, 1996) and two year olds who separate their favourites into those they like to hear and those they like to read for themselves (Baghban, 1984; Taylor and Strickland, 1986). We see siblings with their individual favourites emerging from the same pool of books (Jones, 1996; Wolf and Heath, 1998).

Others have looked specifically at aspects of the relationship between parents, children and favourite books. Robinson and Sulzby (1984) interviewed fifteen parents of children between the ages of two and four who attended a day care centre in Chicago, to gather information about the books parents were reading at home. The study revealed that these parents obtained books from a wide range of sources and that many of the books they chose for their children were not:

> winners of the Caldecott or other such prestigious award. Instead, they ranged from pop-up books to Sesame Street books to Little Golden Books to book club selections. (Robinson and Sulzby, 1984 p57)

Likewise the books which became favourites:

> were not children's classics but were mostly inexpensive, softbound, easily acquired books of the sort found in drugstores or supermarkets. (*ibid*, p.58)

The favourite books were not classics, but they did have 'great personal meaning' (Robinson and Sulzby, 1984 p56). Could it be, they suggested, that parents' memories of their own childhood favourites were being transmitted to their children, or was it some elusive characteristic that our adult eyes cannot see?

Weinberger (1996) studied sixty three year olds from a wide range of social backgrounds. She found that although almost all the children had access to children's books at home, the quantity and choice of books varied widely. Like Robinson and Sulzby (1984), she found that for most children their books were those that were most 'readily available and were relatively cheap' (Weinberger, 1996, p.49). She suspected they were:

> often bought while shopping as an object, together with, or in place of, a small toy or sweets, with the child often initially attracted by a familiar character or logo on the cover. (*ibid*, p49)

She highlighted the differences in the books these children were reading at home with their parents, and the books they would experience when they went to nursery. Indeed, of the two-thirds of children who had favourite books, only eight of these favourites were ones which might be found in a nursery setting. Yet these were books which these children clearly found enriching and stimulating and had made a choice to re-read.

Robinson and Sulzby (1984) found that favourite books have 'great personal meaning' and suggest that there might be a link with either 'elusive characteristics' or parents' 'fond memories' of their own favourite books. Jones (1996) suggested that the affective nature of favourite books is the basis of their power. Perhaps we need to look beyond the specific books themselves to explain their fascination. Perhaps, as Spufford (2002) suggests, if we look at the book, then we are looking in the wrong place. We need to go back to the 'locus of feeling' (Crago, 1979 p144): the reader, and the choices they make *and* the choices that are made for them by their parents.

This was my starting point for exploring the choices made by readers and their parents. Its aim was to examine:

■ the reading choices available to pre-school children at home and the factors involved in the parental selection of books

■ whether parents' own experiences of favourite books impact upon their children's choices

■ parental perceptions about why some books become favourites

Methodology

Graue and Walsh (1998) argue that children *must* be studied in context, not just wider social and cultural context, but in their 'local contexts' of school and home. For although they define 'context' as 'a culturally and historically situated place and time, a specific here and now' (*ibid*, p9), they suggest that children exist within multiple and 'nested' contexts which shape and in turn are shaped by individuals, resources, intentions and ideas. Case studies were conducted of four children and their favourite books within the home setting. I contacted parents I knew in a professional/personal capacity and four agreed to take part in the study.

I wanted the case studies to portray the complex and fluid interaction of events, relationships, and other factors in a unique and real instance and seek to make 'thick descriptions' (Geertz, 1973) of the experiences, thoughts and feelings within each family. Case study is an approach through which 'by study of uniqueness of the particular we come to understand the universal' (Simons, 1996 p231). But here is both the strength *and* the weakness of case study analysis. How far can we generalise from four individual experiences? Bissex (1980) asserts:

> In observing one child we are also observing much that is common to other children. What we cannot know, until we observe others, is how much of what we see is common and how much idiosyncratic. We look for the commonalities, and perhaps overlook the value of the differences. (*ibid*, p173-174)

Data collection involved a series of three semi-structured interviews with each of the parents in their home. Additionally, an interview journal was kept for each child, which recorded my reflections and observations of the interviews and emerging themes. The books available to the children were listed and photographed. Parents also kept a diary in which they recorded the books their children chose over a seven day period.

The first interview involved parents discussing their children's favourite books. The interviews took place wherever the child's books were kept; sitting room or bedroom and sometimes both: we sat together, often on the floor, looking at the books and talking about them. The books were central and served not only as a 'protocol' to informally structure the conversation (Bogdan and Biklen, 1982), but as a trigger to memories and provided a rich source of discussion. The second interview was to check and probe my interpretation of the themes which had emerged from the first. So we sat, often side-by-side, and worked through the interpretation I had made. Working from analysis summary sheets I had produced, the themes were discussed one at a time, points were clarified and agreed upon.

We also talked about the diary they had kept and how or whether what had been recorded fitted into those earlier themes. The diaries simply recorded which books had been read by their child, by whom and who had made the choice. Parents were free to record the information in any way they chose and to add any additional comments as they felt appropriate. Photographs of bookcases and piles of books, together with the lists of books available to each child, were studied and used as data and so the camera itself became a data-gathering technique and the books artifacts (Bogdan and Biklen, 1982). I then analysed all of this data using inductive coding techniques (Strauss, 1987) to determine themes and patterns.

From this drawing-out of patterns, themes and the unique moments from the data and then relating these back to the original research questions, a vignette for each case study was constructed. Vignettes tell a story that illustrate a particular interpretation, a recounted version through which an interpretive perspective is threaded (Graue and Walsh, 1998). I sought to create a vignette which 'fitted' with each parent's lived experience, a vignette which captured the complex relationship each child had with their favourite books and yet was plausible, relatable and trustworthy. But however closely each parent felt the vignette 'fitted' with their lived experience, it remains my interpretation and therefore can be only one interpretation.

At the third interview I presented each parent with a draft of the vignette I had written about them and their child and I asked them to consider three issues: Was it an accurate interpretation, was it a fair interpretation, and what ought to be changed? All the parents agreed that the vignettes were an accurate representation of the data. With the exception of one minor amendment, the only alteration we made to the vignettes was to change the names.

Findings

Space precludes the presentation of the vignettes but the following profiles contain brief details of each of the children, all of them white:

■ Harriet is aged two years and ten months. She lives with both her parents and her five year old brother. Her first language is English and her parents define themselves as middle class.

■ Oliver is aged one year and ten months. He lives with both his parents and has no siblings. His first language is English and his parents define themselves as working class.

■ Paige is aged two years and ten months. She lives with both her parents and has no siblings. Her first language is English and her parents define themselves as working class.

■ William is aged two years and two months. He lives with both his parents and his four year old brother. His first language is English and his parents define themselves as middle class.

Range of available books

All four children had access to a large range of books, from simple 'point and label' books to contemporary classics such as *Where's Spot* (Hill, 2000) and *The Very Hungry Caterpillar* (Carle, 1974). The size of the collections ranged from 114 books to 159, the median was 142. Although all the children had some access to books which might be described as 'classics', this varied among the four collections and many of the books were not part of the established canon of children's literature. Few of those books that parents identified as favourites could be described as classics – only four of the thirteen favourite books were titles which would be stocked by a library or bookshop. Each book collection was highly individual and unique. Likewise, the favourite books were also highly individual and represented a range of book genres (see Appendix 1).

All the children had more than one favourite book. Only Oliver's mother felt that she could identify his most favourite book. Some of the children seemed to have phases when they were particularly engaged with a set of books and would then move onto new ones, but there remained a core of books which were long-standing favourites and to which they returned. There were discernible patterns within some of the children's favourite books; Oliver's favourites were about transport and Harriet's favourites were interactive. But the comic-book style of William's favourites applied to only four out of five, and the odd one out had been his favourite over the longest period. There was no discernible pattern to any of Paige's favourites.

Sources for books

Parents used a range of sources to obtain books for their children: bookshops; book-clubs; supermarkets; departmental stores; second-hand bookshops, car boot sales, library sales, family and friends. All parents were opportunistic in that if they came across children's books in the course of their day, they would check to see anything caught their eye. Oliver's mother always checked the book-club's selection at the hairdresser's and Paige's mother chose a present from the newsagent on the way home after a day out alone:

> so instead of taking her sweets and things, I thought I'll get her a few books. I knew she liked nursery rhymes but she didn't actually have a book with all the nursery rhymes in. That was only 99p so I thought I'd get her that.

Contrary to Weinberger's (1996) 'suspicion' that such books were often bought haphazardly while shopping, these parents made definite and conscious decisions about the books they chose for their children.

Factors involved in parental selection

Parents drew on their extensive knowledge of their child's unique interests, their 'learned understanding' (Robinson, 1983) of, for example, Oliver's fascination with transport, Harriet's need for books with which she can physically engage, William's enjoyment of busy pictures, where he can find and point things out and Paige's interest in bears and nursery rhymes. Parents focused on whether or not the book engaged their child's particular interests.

They also drew on their own personal experience of books and reading in general. Paige's mother used her experiences as a nursery nurse to inform her choices,

> It comes from my experiences, what I like and what I know other children have liked.

William's mother enjoyed introducing and using books she had as a child,

> If you enjoyed it when you were younger you think, I wonder if my children will enjoy it too. I just remember annuals more than anything else.

Oliver's mother looked for a particular sense of 'flow' within a story,

> A good story flows, it reads well. I think if you read it and it flows, you're more into it and you want to keep reading it until you've finished it. That's what I'm like with my books.

Harriet's mother had a more pragmatic engagement with books,

> I don't collect books, I buy them for a purpose.

It was each parents' unique relationship with books and their individual experience of what already worked with their child, which defined whether it might possibly be a 'good' book.

The impact of parents' own experiences of favourite books

Parents mostly had little recollection of favourite books from their early childhood. They felt that the impact of their childhood experiences of reading had been more important than actual books they had read. They remembered their own reading experiences, specific memories about where books had been kept or visits to the library with their own parents, but there were few 'fond memories' (Robinson and Sulzby, 1984) of books.

Only William's mother felt that specific childhood books had made an impact on her child's choices. She was also the only one who had kept books from her pre-school childhood. But it wasn't the books themselves that she remembered, but the images and colours:

> I remember the pictures. It's funny that it's the picture that I actually remember.

Annuals were an important part of her early childhood reading and so she introduced them to William, initially by buying new annuals each year and recently by using her own childhood annuals.

> I always remember liking the annuals. I started buying them because I remembered liking them myself.

William's mother has also noticed how this enjoyment of annuals has transferred to the types of children's books both she and William seem to prefer: a comic book format:

> where the story flows through and you can see different parts of the story on the same page.

Here then was one child whose mother's 'fond memories' may have had an impact on the reading choices he makes.

How parents identified books as 'favourites'
Parents used an array of indicators to define what 'favourite' meant.

- ■ *self-selection*. Parents felt that a favourite book was one which their child had made a conscious decision to engage with, one the child had selected his/herself by fetching a particular book to read, pointing to a book on a shelf, or flicking through their books, studying their covers before choosing.

- ■ *physical markers of love*. Parents felt that favourite books bore the physical evidence of their love: their appearance indicated a special relationship. These books were particularly chewed or broken, often heavily sellotaped or in several pieces. The books which held favourite images fell open naturally at specific pages and these images were sometimes covered in sticky fingerprints or had pieces of biscuit stuck to the page.

- ■ *requests for repetition*. The repeated request to read a particular book over and over again was seen by parents to be an indicator of something special. But this was not just children simply asking

'Again, again' or even requesting the same book at every reading session. It was also a physical action: turning the book back to the beginning or simply refusing to accept a parent's next choice of book by tossing it aside and reinstating their own choice.

■ *responses to books.* These were the idiosyncratic responses that certain books produced: attention – the particular way in which their child would sit and listen to a book; interaction – the unique way their child would interact with aspects of a book; and emotional – the way their child would react to a favourite book with a facial expression, a special 'giddiness', or a particular attentiveness. Parents knew that a book was special if their children had selected it themselves or if they repeatedly requested it, or if it was particularly damaged, but ultimately it was a child's idiosyncratic response to a book which determined whether it was a favourite:

> It's the expression on his face.
>
> It's posture, it's concentration, it's whether the eyes are in the right place.
>
> The laughing and the giggling.
>
> She's very, very quiet and intent on listening.

These parents used their insider knowledge of their children to determine which specific books within large and varied book collections were in fact favourites.

What made it a favourite book?

For Oliver's mother, his fascination for transport books, and diggers in particular, comes from his ability to *relate* it to his immediate experience. Diggers are part of his everyday experience

> We listen for them. When I hear them coming I go, 'listen' and his face lights up with excitement.

Oliver's mother believes that his excitement comes from simply *finding* a favourite image and *knowing* what it is.

> He picks it up because he knows what's in it. He knows what he's looking for.

William's mother also identified this sense of excitement at *finding and knowing* and also described another aspect of *knowing*, the sense of knowing what's going to happen next, of anticipation.

> He'll sit very quietly and then all of a sudden he can't contain himself, like two or three pages before the sheep start squelching through the muck, he'll start going, 'slurp, slurp' and he'll start laughing and giggling.

Harriet's favourite books are those with which she wants to engage and it is this motivation to engage physically with these books that Harriet's mother identifies as being important.

> She doesn't display enough understanding of vocabulary or valuing vocabulary to want a book for any other reason. She can't hold a story in her head yet, so it has to be something beyond the narrative.

But Harriet's mother doesn't attribute the importance of *beyond the narrative* to just Harriet:

> It's all to do with doing, it's not to do with interaction that much, it's not to do with communication that much, it's to do with them doing and exploring. Maybe to a large degree the book has to be worth exploring.

Paige's mother finds it very difficult to say why specific books are favourites. But she recognises that Paige has two distinct *types* of favourite, those which she likes to read to herself and those which she chooses to experience with her mother, new titles or those which require a particular rehearsed interaction and, always hovering between the two types are those 'in-between' books – books which are :

> actually easy stories and she's quite familiar with them, but she still needs me to read them to her.

Paige's mother believes that Paige's two types of favourite books are sometimes fulfilling a different need, for comfort and sometimes for challenge.

Conclusions

All four children had experience of a wide range of books. They chose their favourites from a large collection of books, many of which had been selected with each child's interests and preferences in mind. There was some indication in the study that parents' 'fond memories' of their favourites might be communicated to their children. However, there was also an indication that a mother's lived experience of reading may be a factor in the choices they make for their children. For each individual has her own particular literate history (Meek, 1980), a unique collection of memories and experiences which inform the choices she makes for herself and her children. This also includes a learned understanding of her children's engagement with books and their interests and affective responses to books. Some parents clearly put their own choices in the context of a wider understanding of what their children chose to read for themselves.

These parents recognised favourite books through a range of indicators: self-selection, physical markers of love, requests for repetition and idiosyncratic responses to books. It was this idiosyncratic response of attention, interaction and emotion which revealed to parents a particular book's 'great personal meaning' (Robinson and Sulzby, 1984) and which gave them their status as 'favourites', although that meaning was not always easy to identify. They had that vague and imprecise 'something', which drew each child back to them time and time again, a something which was often 'beyond the narrative'. It was more than words or pictures and it was different for each child. For these parents, it was about relatability, the joy of finding and knowing, the books being worth exploring, and the tension between comfort and challenge. These were books which had great personal meaning, books which these children chose to engage with repeatedly and whose emotional involvement gave them so much pleasure. These books were embedded in the private context of each child's world. Their status as favourite books was defined by this personal meaning and displayed by each child's idiosyncratic and emotional response.

The favourite books themselves inevitably draw us back to the thorny question of 'quality' and what counts as a 'good book'. Is a good book that which is determined by academics, critics or reviewers, or is it as Moss (1977) suggests, to be assessed only 'by the light it brings to a child's eye' (*ibid*, p142)? Despite having access to books which might be described by some as contemporary classics, only four of the thirteen favourite books fell within the established canon of children's literature. Yet all the books vibrated with personal significance and preference. They were favourites because these parents could see the light it brought to their child's eye. These children remind us that the concept of quality relies heavily upon the subjective and idiosyncratic interaction a child has with a particular book. This means that potentially a 'quality' reading experience can come from the interaction between a child and *any* text. It is simply unhelpful to adopt a negative, deficit model of children's reading choices (Hall and Coles, 1999), for this disregards the value of a particular book to an individual. We may not always understand the meaning a particular book has for a child but we should most certainly value it!

Areas For Further Study

This study has revealed tantalising glimpses of the possible impact of parents' literate experiences on the choices they make for their children and the choices children make for themselves. It also reveals how little we know about what appears to be a complex relationship between a parent's literate past, their literate present and their learned understanding of their child's interests. Until the dearth of empirical research into pre-school reading choices is addressed, we cannot know how much the study is common to all children and how much is idiosyncratic. These are just the favourite books of four children. The factors involved in parental selection, the indicators of their children's favourites and their perceptions about why particular books are favourites are just the views of four parents. In fact they are the views of four mothers, for the study did not include fathers, siblings or wider family members. What impact do they have on a child's reading choices and do children have particular favourites that they share with particular family members? Further studies might look at this imbalance. Nor do we know how favourite books might progress through a child's life. Further study might explore the part favourite books play in defining what literacy and literature mean to a child and their contribution towards a child's early literacy development. This study was only ever an exploration of the notion of favourite books: there is so much more for us to learn.

References

Agnew, K. (1996) "You're not wasting your money on that!' – a bookseller's view' in M Styles, E Bearne and V Watson (eds) *Voices Off: Texts, Contexts and Readers* London: Cassell

Baghban, M. (1984) *Our Daughter Learns to Read and Write: A case study from birth to three* Newark: International Reading Association

Bettelheim, B. and Zelan, K. (1982) *On Learning to Read* London: Thames and Hudson

Bissex, G. L. (1980) *Gnys at Wrk: A Child Learns to Write and Read* Cambridge, MA: Harvard University Press

Bogdan, R. C. and Biklen, S. K. (1982) *Qualitative Research for Education: An introduction to theory and methods* Boston: Allyn and Bacon

Butler, D. (1979) *Cushla and her books* London: Hodder and Stoughton

Butler, D. (1995) *Babies Need Books* (3rd edn) Harmondsworth: Penguin

Campbell, R. (1999) *Literacy from Home to School: Reading with Alice* Stoke-on-Trent: Trentham Books

Carle, E. (1974) *The Very Hungry Caterpillar* Harmondsworth: Picture Puffin

Crago, H. (1979) 'Cultural categories and the criticism of children's literature' *Signal* 30 pp.140-150

Crago, M. and Crago, H. (1983) *Prelude to Literacy* Illinois: Illinois University Press

Geertz, C. (ed) (1973) *The Interpretation of Cultures* New York: Basic Books

Gopnik, A., Meltzoff, A. and Kuhl, P. (2000) *How Babies Think* London: Weidenfeld and Nicholson

Graue, M. E. and Walsh, D. J. (1998) *Studying Children in Context: Theories, Methods, and Ethics* London: Sage Publications

Hall, C. and Coles, M. (1999) *Children's Reading Choices* London: Routledge

Hill, E. (2000) *Where's Spot?* London: Frederick Warne

Holdaway, D. (1979) *The Foundations of Literacy* Sydney: Ashton Scholastic

Jones, R. (1996) *Emerging Patterns of Literacy* London: Routledge

Meek, M. (1980) 'Prolegomena: for a study of children's literature' in M Benton (ed) *Approaches to Research in Children's Literature* Southampton: University of Southampton Department of Education

Millard, E. (1997) *Differently Literate: Boys, Girls and the Schooling of Literacy* London: Falmer Press

Minns, H. (1997) *Read it to me now! Learning at home and at school* (2nd edn) Buckingham: OUP.

Moss, E. (1977) 'The 'Peppermint' lesson' in M Meek, A Warlow, and G Barton (eds) *The Cool Web: The Pattern of Children's Reading* London: Bodley Head

Nutbrown, C. (2000) 'Alex's Story' in E. Millard (ed) (2000) *Enquiring into Literacy* Sheffield: Department of Educational Studies, University of Sheffield pp. 23-42

Robinson, F. (1983) Parents Descriptions of Young Children's Behaviors toward Favorite Books MA thesis, Northwestern University ERIC Document ED 230 910

Robinson, F. and Sulzby, E. (1984) 'Parents, children, and 'favorite' books: An interview study' in J A Niles and LA Harris (eds) *33rd Yearbook of the National Reading Conference* Rochester NY: National Reading Conference

Simons, H. (1996) 'The paradox of case study' *Cambridge Journal of Education,* Vol 26, 2: 225-240

Spufford, F. (2002) *The Child that Books Built* London: Faber and Faber

Stake, R. E. (1994) 'Case studies' in N K Denzin and Y S Lincoln (eds) *Handbook of Qualitative Research* London: Sage

Strauss, A. L. (1987) *Qualitative analysis for social scientists.* New York, NY: Cambridge University Press

Taylor, D. and Strickland, D. S. (1986) *Family Storybook Reading* Portsmouth NH: Heinemann

Waterland, L. (1985) *Read With Me: An Apprenticeship Approach to Reading* Stroud, Glos.: Thimble Press

Watson, V. (1992) 'Irresponsible writers and responsible readers' in M Styles, E. Bearne and V. Watson (eds) *After Alice: Exploring Children's Literature* London: Cassell

Weinberger, J. (1996) *Literacy Goes to School* London: Paul Chapman Publishing

White, D. (1954) *Books Before Five* New Zealand Council for Educational Research

Whitehead, M. (1999) *Supporting Language and Literacy Development in the Early Years* Buckingham: OUP

Wolf, S. A. and Heath, S. B. (1998) 'Living in a world of words' in H. Jenkins (ed) *The Children's Culture Reader* New York: New York University Press

Appendix 1: Four children's favourite books

Harriet
Cousins L (1990) *Maisie Goes Swimming* London: Walker Books

Lorenz Books (1998) *Point and Say Animal Friends* London: Lorenz Books

McKee D (1996) *Elmer's Pop-Up Book* London: Andersen Press

Nielson C and Steer D (1999) *Snappy Little Movers* St. Helen's: The Book People Ltd

Paige
Egmont Books Ltd (2001) *Thomas Selection Box* London: Egmont Books Ltd

Index Direct Book Supplies (1998) *The Wheels On The Bus* Northants: Index Direct Book Supplies

Oliver
Dean Books (2000) *Gordon In Trouble* London: Dean

Michael O'Mara Books (2000) *Baby's World* London: Michael O'Mara Books

William
Alborough J (1999) *Balloon* London: Collins Picture Lions

Alborough J (2000) *Duck in the Truck* London: Collins Picture Lions

Awdry C and Stott K (1993) *Learn with Thomas* London: Dean

IPC Magazines Ltd (1974) *Walt Disney's Donald and Mickey Annual 1975* London: IPC Magazines Ltd

Random House (2000) *Pipkin's Rainbow* London: Random House

13

Is it OK to play? Perceptions of play in a small rural primary school

Jan Christmas

Overview

The importance of integrating play into the curriculum has widespread support from early years educators, and is now enshrined in the government document *Curriculum guidance for the Foundation Stage* (QCA, 2000). This belief is substantiated by the wealth of research available on how children learn, and the benefits of play as a tool for learning. Practitioners cannot always articulate the reasons for integrating play into the curriculum, to share what we know with other participants in the process, parents, colleagues and children. This risks the accusation of 'eulogising play' (Anning, 1997 p31) and deprives practitioners of the support and understanding needed to make children's learning successful.

As a new member of staff and the only Foundation Stage teacher in the school, I wanted to find out whether parents and staff shared my views on the importance of a 'play-based curriculum' (Wood and Bennett, 1997 p22). I hoped that by involving the parents and staff in my research, we could begin to raise the status of play in the setting and establish a basis for staff development needs and closer co-operation with parents.

> Quality evaluation is essentially a value-based enterprise, it is best achieved through the active involvement of participants in the process. (Pascal and Bertram, 1994 p162)

The study involved finding out, through questionnaires and interviews, what parents in the reception class and colleagues already knew about learning through play, and how this compared to the literature on a play-based curriculum.

Learning through play

For the purposes of the study, which took place in a school, I defined learning through play as play which has educational consequences, children learning through 'playful experiences' (Moyles, 2002 p2). Many of the theories about learning through play that appear in current practice are based on the work of the early educationists and philosophers. An awareness of the origins of 'the early childhood tradition' (Wood and Attfield, 1996 p16) can help us to understand how we arrived at current views and practice, and possibly to anticipate what might happen in the future.

Until the 1800s, children were seen as small adults; Rousseau began the identification of the importance of play, continued by Froebel, Montessori and Steiner, and the early British pioneers Susan Isaacs and Margaret McMillan. Tassoni and Hucker see all of Froebel's ideas reflected today, in the use of finger rhymes and songs, in 'child-centred' education, and in the emphasis placed on 'children experiencing things and discovering for themselves' (Tassoni and Hucker, 2000 p16). Anning feels that Steiner has given us

> ...the intense concern for the individual child..., the slightly fey approach of some infant teachers to the 'mystery and wonder' of childhood and the Plowdenesque notion that 'at the heart of education lies the child'. (Anning, 1997 p13)

Isaacs' ideas, of seeing free-flow play as a way of integrating learning, of parents as important educators, of using observations to develop her understanding of children's intellectual growth, seem to underpin 'the ideologies of many infant teachers in the 1990s' (Anning, 1997 p15). Moyles (2002) argues that we need to justify play in an educational context. Her model of how children learn through play is derived from Bruner's work on learning and Hutt's classification of play (Hutt, 1979).

> Exploratory play/enactive learning ... leads to... acquiring knowledge/skills.
>
> Creative play/iconic learning ... leads to ... using knowledge/skills.
>
> Problem solving play/symbolic learning ... leads to ... enrichment, extension, practice, revision. (Moyles, 2002 p4)

Tassoni and Hucker (2000) justify the role of play as a tool for learning by making it the central focus and link between each of five single areas of a child's development (emotional, language, cognitive, physical and social). David articulates what early years' educators may instinctively feel about learning through play:

> During play, children are free to make choices and to follow interests, are self-motivated, engage in play about what is relevant to themselves and their lives, dare to take risks, learn from mistakes without any fear of failure, and negotiate and set their own goals and challenges. (David, 1992 p78)

If we see parents as the child's first and most important educators, it is crucial to share our knowledge and understanding about how children learn with them, particularly about learning through play. The Scottish Consultative Council states:

> When staff and parents work together to support children's learning, it can have significant positive effects on the way in which children value themselves and those around them. (Scottish CCC, 1999 p52)

Similarly, Tassoni and Hucker's view is that working together has 'measurable and long-lasting effects on achievement' (Tassoni and Hucker, 2000 p40). If we accept this as true, it is essential that we involve parents in our theories and practices about play. This sharing increases the value and self-esteem of what they are doing and has implications for the child. Sayeed and Guerin see the parents' involvement in and 'clear understanding' of their role as enriching their child's play 'in any given context' (Sayeed and Guerin, 2000, p.20).

The Education Reform Act had a great influence on play in reception classes. Although reception classes have never been included in the National Curriculum, the downward pressure to prepare our reception children for Key Stage One was felt by many teachers. Keating *et al* claim that until this time 'play held a central place... in the curriculum of the early years', although 'its position in the reception class was slightly more contentious' (Keating *et al,* 2000 p438). The importance of play was emphasised in the large number of books and articles being published, and 'many of us were convinced that the battle for play was won' (*ibid*, p438).

However, the introduction in 1989 of a National Curriculum for five to eleven year olds, with its specific emphasis on learning outcomes, gave practitioners, including headteachers, the feeling that play would have to lose its place as 'a major feature of the early years curriculum', in order to 'adapt practice to meet statutory requirements' (Hamilton, 1996 p28). There was concern that the 'commitment to play as the principal means of learning in early childhood' would be eroded, particularly for four year olds in reception classes, because of the 'negative downward impact' of the National Curriculum (Wood, 1999 p11). This was in spite of the report of the Rumbold Committee who had endorsed play as having

> ...a fundamental role in early childhood education, supplying the foundation upon which learning is built. (DES, 1990 p11)

Increasing numbers of four year olds, some of them within a few days of their fourth birthday, were being admitted to reception classes and with the already overloaded curriculum this meant that

> Reception Class teachers were often isolated in their battle to maintain good Early Years practice against this downward pressure of the more formal Programmes of Study. (Keating *et al*, 2002 p4)

Headteachers' worries about Ofsted inspections and the later introduction of the literacy and numeracy strategies intensified the pressure. Katz describes similar pressure to teach young children in America the 'basics of literacy and numeracy as 'a sort of academic boot camp approach to teaching'! (Katz, 2001 p2) Since then, reception teachers have been offered more flexibility within those strategies, but at the time it was argued that such pressure meant that

> ...policy makers and practitioners had consequently lost sight of the whole concept of what constitutes an effective and appropriate Early Years Curriculum. (Keating *et al*, 2002 p4)

1996 saw the publication of the government document *Desirable Learning Outcomes*, (DfEE/SCAA, 1996) which set out minimum goals for children's learning, on entering compulsory education at five years of age. Unfortunately this did not help the reception teacher, who now had to cope with the possibility of each child's changing from the *Desirable Learning Outcomes* to the National Curriculum on his/her fifth birthday! The introduction of baseline assessment, in 1997, to take place in a child's first term at school, which was not consistent from one local authority to another, was seen by many as another means of formalising 'the top down influence' of the National Curriculum (Wood, 1999 p22).

In 1999, the *Desirable Learning Outcomes* were reviewed by the Qualifications and Curriculum Authority and a new Foundation Stage, extending the early years curriculum to the end of the reception year, was created. For the first time, official government curriculum guidance endorsed play as a 'key way in which young children learn' (QCA, 2000 p25). This has been widely welcomed by early years practitioners as a step in the right direction.

Reception teachers now had the opportunity and challenge of implementing those principles into what they and the whole school, including staff and parents, saw as acceptable or best practice. As the new reception teacher in my school, it was also a good starting point for me to begin to formulate our policy on learning through play. By involving parents and staff in my research, we could work together so that we could all enhance our knowledge and share in the ownership of the final policy.

Methodological issues
The context, participants and methods

My school is a small village school of fewer than 120 children, with a total complement of six full and part-time teachers, a headteacher, a nursery nurse and four classroom assistants. In such a small community, it is crucial to work together as a team, and I wanted to involve the whole team in my research. Consequently, I chose to interview every member of staff individually, everyone was asked the same questions.

I wanted to know 'what do parents *in the reception class* and staff know about learning through play?' I had sixteen children in the class and asked all their parents to express their opinions honestly, in anonymous questionnaires.

I was able to hand out most of the questionnaires for parents in person, except to the four children who went home on the school bus, whose questionnaires were placed in their bags. Having promised anonymity, I took no note of who had returned the questionnaires, so could not remind parents about the final date for return, but I did put up a notice asking for completed questionnaires to be returned by a certain date. Twelve were returned by that date, which was to be the final total. The numbers were small and the higher rate of return was from the parents I had approached personally. All the staff agreed to be interviewed at a place and time of their choice. All participants were assured of confidentiality and anonymity and gave their consent before the research began. I provided feedback for participants at the end of the study by giving them a brief written summary.

Key findings

The following four questions were used in both the interviews with staff and the questionnaires with parents:

Do you think play is important for young children? Please say why.

What role do you think parents have during children's play?

What role do you think the school staff has during children's play?

Do you think children learn from play?

Interview and questionnaires were coded and categorised in order to identify key themes from perspectives of staff and parents.

Staff views

All the staff regarded play as important for children's development and identified three areas towards which 'playful experiences' (Moyles, 2002 p2) would contribute: learning skills, developing imagination and skill for life.

Seven out of eleven staff valued the roles of teacher and parent equally. This is important for two reasons; that parents are valued as their child's educators, 'the most significant people in his/her environment' (Bruce, 1991 p15), and that being 'a player' and being 'playful' is a valued activity (Moyles, 2002 p4).

The role of staff in children's play (question 3), on the other hand, was seen as predominantly a teaching one, including directing, structuring and planning for play. One respondent agreed with Bennett *et al* (1997) that observation of play was a useful tool for assessment. Partnership between staff and children in play was only mentioned in three responses, contrary to research which has identified this as crucial for staff. The response may reflect the few staff with early years training and/or experience.

Asking whether children learn through play elicited a positive response from everyone, though seven of the eleven interviewees did not say how this learning occurs. This finding supports Anning's view that early years educators have traditionally supported play in the curriculum 'without recognising the origins of their beliefs' (Anning, 1997 p6). However, all of them readily identified examples of play from five areas of learning.

On the whole the interviews showed that the staff valued play and its contribution to learning both at home and at school. They also valued parents' contribution to their children's education, particularly when joining in with play. The staff role, on the other hand, was seen as primarily a teaching one, with little identification of supporting and extending unstructured play. Although they could describe 'learning through play' experiences, most did not articulate how children learn through these experiences, or express how they valued play as a tool for learning.

Parents' views

Parents supported the idea of play as important for children's learning. Their reasons fell into six categories, three which matched the staff's reasons but also three more: for fun, for health (mental and physical), and for 'letting off steam'.

Asked about parents' role in play, the highest number of responses identified the parent as partner in their children's play, showing an understanding that 'children find it easier to play if they are supported by an adult' (Gura, 1992 p17). The partner's role is generally referred to as 'joining in' and is not developed further, except for one comment, 'to join in if required, and leave alone if not!' This is a reminder of Bruce's advice not to take an interest in the child's play unless invited (Bruce, 2001 pp86-89). In contrast, the staff as partner in play rated only two responses, again 'joining in', which shows that parents saw this as a low priority, unlike advice for practitioners (Moyles, 2002 p4; Tassoni and Hucker, 2001 pp80-81), in which interaction with children is seen as a key skill.

The role of 'parent as teacher' had only half the number of responses as that of 'staff as teacher'. It would appear that this group of parents see the staff much more as educators than they see themselves. This has implications for the early years' co-ordinator and the school, to share their thinking that parents are significant in learning. The other major role for staff, according to parents' responses, is to supervise children's behaviour, or to teach them to behave appropriately, but few identified this role for themselves. Perhaps good behaviour is perceived as more important in school, as a prerequisite for learning because learning only takes place when you are well-behaved.

When asked 'Do you think children learn from play?' all parents were positive, and four went on to say how they thought this learning took place. One of these is close to Moyles' reason for playing (Moyles, 1989): 'it keeps their minds active'. The examples given of their own child's play covered all six areas of learning in QCA's *Curriculum Guidance for the Foundation Stage* (2000), which illustrates an holistic view of learning from the parents.

From their responses to the questionnaire, this group of parents valued play both at home and at school, and understood how children learned and could be taught through play. The school staff's role was seen as an educator in an educational situation, whereas the parent's role was seen as a partner in spontaneous play and, to a lesser extent, as an educator.

Overall Findings

All the respondents thought that play was important for children, and that children learned through play. Although all recognised the parents' role in their child's education, staff responses were weighted towards the staff as educator/ teacher, and the parent as a partner in play. Parents had a broader range of reasons for the importance of play, including fun. Does this say something about today's educators and the current education system?

We might expect school staff to know more about learning through play and to value it more, because of their training and experience. Yet, in this case study at least, the findings indicate that their perspectives were much the same as those of the parents. This could be explained in part by the staff's sharing of their views of play during home visits, the initial parents' meeting, the school handbook and displays. It might also be because the parents at the school show an active interest in their children's education.

There was little evidence of respondents' ideas of how children learn or how they learn through play. In the case of the staff, does this reflect the content of teacher training and professional development, or is it that teachers often had difficulty in 'making their implicit theories explicit'? (Bennett *et al*, 1997 p132)

Conclusion

For the school itself, the study showed that the parents and staff supported play through learning in the reception class, although their knowledge of the theories behind it and of the adult's role within it could benefit from further development. This could be an area for professional development for staff and for parent workshops, and possibly a role for the early years co-ordinator. Whether such small-scale research has implications for the wider community is debatable; the school is not unique, but neither is it typical in size or setting. The findings reflect other research (Moyles and Adams, 2001; Bennett *et al*, 1997) in that

> ...while we declared our whole hearted commitment to the value of play, there was little clarity or substance in our understanding of the role of the practitioner in planning for, assessing and developing children's learning in this way. (Moyles and Adams, 2001 p3)

This has implications outside the school, for teacher training, for professional development and for government policy which, with the Early Learning Goals, seems to acknowledge the value of play as integral to the needs of young children.

So is it OK to play? Adults in this case study appear to believe that play is important for children's learning, but the belief alone is not enough to sustain its central place in the early years curriculum. As early years educators, we also need to be continually evaluating, updating and reflecting on our understanding of and commitment to play. This is particularly pertinent in the reception class, since 'it is still not fully recognised that reception children have the same needs as their nursery-aged peers' (Keating *et al*, 2002 p18). If we are to move forward, we must be able to articulate our theories and share the message with all the adults involved in the educative process, for the sake of the children at the heart of the process. For them, we must ensure that it is indeed OK to play.

References

Anning, A. (1997) *The First Years at School.* Buckingham: Open University Press

Bennett, N., Wood, L. and Rogers, S. (1997) *Teaching through Play.* Buckingham: Open University Press

Bruce, T. (1991) *Time to Play in Early Childhood Education.* London: Hodder and Stoughton

Bruce, T. (2001) *Learning through play: Babies, Toddlers and the Foundation Years.* London: Hodder and Stoughton

David, T. (1992) 'Curriculum in the Early Years', in Pugh, G. (ed.), *Contemporary Issues in the Early Years.* London: Paul Chapman

DES (1990) *The Education of Children Under Five,* London: HMSO

DfEE/SCAA (1996) *Desirable outcomes of Nursery Education on entry to compulsory schooling,* London: SCAA

Gura, P. (ed.) (1992) *Exploring Learning. Young Children and Blockplay.* London: Paul Chapman

Hamilton, S. (1996), 'Changing the Focus of Play'. *Primary Practice,* No.3, pp28-32

Hutt, C. (1979), 'Play in the under 5s; form, development and function', in Howells, J.G. (ed.) *Modern Perspectives in the Psychiatry of Infancy.* New York: Bruner

Katz, L. (2001), in Patten, P. *Lessons from a Longtime – and Much-Travelled – Teacher Educator: An Interview with Lilian Katz* (ON-LINE – http://npin.org. pnews/2001/pnew301/feat301.html).

Keating, I., Basford, J., Hodson, E. and Harnett, A. (2002) *Reception Teacher Responses to the Foundation Stage,* (ON-LINE – i.keating@mmu.ac.uk).

Keating, I., Fabian, H., Jordan, P., Mavers, D. and Roberts, J. (2000), 'Well, I've not done any work today. I don't know why I came to school.' Perceptions of Play in the Reception Class'. *Educational Studies,* Vol. 26, No. 4, pp437-454

Moyles, J. (2002) *Playing and Learning,* presentation to Grimsby and District Early Years Association

Moyles, J. and Adams, S. (2001) *StEPs, Statements of Entitlement to Play* Buckingham: Open University Press

Nutbrown, C. (1999) (2nd edition) *Threads of Thinking* London: Paul Chapman.

Pascal, C. and Bertram, T. (1994) 'Evaluating and improving the quality of play', in Moyles, J. (ed.) *The Excellence of Play* Buckingham: Open University Press

QCA (2000) *Curriculum Guidance for the Foundation Stage* London: QCA.

Sayeed, Z. and Guerin, E. (2000) *Early Years Play. A Happy Medium for Assessment and Intervention.* London: David Fulton

Scottish Consultative Council on the Curriculum (1999) *Curriculum Framework for Children 3 to 5.* Dundee: The Scottish Office

Tassoni, P. and Hucker, K. (2000) *Planning Play and the Early Years.* Heinemann: Oxford

Wood, E. (1999) 'The impact of the National Curriculum on play in reception classes'. *Educational Research* Vol. 41, No.1, Spring 1999, pp.11-22

Wood, E. and Attfield, J. (1996) *Play, Learning and the Early Childhood Curriculum.* London: Paul Chapman

14

Supporting children's thinking skills in the Foundation Stage

Heather Davies

Introduction

The development of thinking skills is supported by theories of cognition that see learners as active constructors of their own knowledge and frameworks of interpretation (McGuiness, 1999). Children are supported in this through interactions with 'knowledgeable others' within a socio-cultural context (Vygotsky, 1978). One of the principle characteristics of a learner is the capacity to think, a view articulated within the rationale of the 'thinking skills movement' promoted by Fisher (1998) and others. Government initiatives have begun to recognise that the challenge for effective schools is to combine the acquisition of knowledge with the development of children's thinking (Blunkett, 2000).

Principles embedded in the National Curriculum reflect this move, advocating that by using thinking skills, children can focus on 'knowing how' as well as 'knowing what' or 'learning how to learn'. The importance of the development of such skills is also recognised in early childhood; practitioners are encouraged to provide opportunities for children to solve problems, make decisions, predict and question, in a variety of contexts in the learning environment. (DfEE/QCA, 2000).

This chapter reports an exploratory study of how practitioners in one Foundation Stage setting supported children's development of thinking skills, through talk and the use of non-verbal communication during planned activities. The study focused on learning and teaching inter-actions between four practitioners with different backgrounds, roles and training, from head teacher to PGCE student, and children in a nursery school setting, during different types of planned activities over one school term.

Supporting children's thinking skills
Scaffolding and guided participation
Scaffolding is associated with adult/child interaction in the zone of proximal development (Vygotsky, 1978). The term has its roots within the sociocultural approach to teaching and learning (Vygotsky, 1962), where cognitive development is seen as resulting from interaction with those who are more advanced learners, and is a metaphor for the process by which an adult assists a child to carry out a task which is just beyond his/her capabilities. Rogoff's (1990) view that cognitive development results from children's participation in adult-guided activities, ('guided participation'), parallels that of scaffolding. Key features of adult prac-tice include structuring learning situations for the child and eventually transferring responsibility for that learning to them.

Practitioners' questioning of children
Mercer (1994), in adopting the neo-Vygotskian principles of scaffolding and guided participation, places the role of talk centrally, '...an analysis of the process of teaching and learning, of constructing knowledge, must be an analysis of language in use.' (p6)

Questioning is a key strategy for adults in eliciting children's current knowledge. Wood and Wood (1983) classify questions according to the level of cognitive demand placed on the learner. High level questions demand, for example, explanation, interpretation and the formulation of hypotheses, medium level questions require labels, descriptions and the use of recall, whilst low level or closed questioning encourages limited responses such as 'yes' or 'no'.

Wood (1986) argues that if teachers' repeatedly ask questions it is a counter-productive strategy for trying to find out what children know or are thinking, as the more teachers question, the less children say.

Non-questioning turns and non-verbal prompts
If talk supports thinking, children need to be encouraged to engage in conversation. If questions are not effective, adults need to find other means of generating children's interest and engagement. Wood *et al*

(1980) suggest that children's involvement in a conversation can be sustained by the adult's personal contributions, such as giving an opinion or reflecting back to the children what they are doing or seeing. These non-questioning turns provide a springboard for the children's own commentaries and questions, as well as allowing them to learn how to use language to structure thought.

Talk, then, is fundamental to the process of scaffolding learning but so too are non-verbal prompts such as gestures, pauses and eye contact (Rogoff, 1990).

Modelling metacognitive processes

Metacognition, the ability to observe and monitor one's cognitive behaviour, needs to be modelled by the adult, before such self-awareness is internalised by the child. Talk is also the vehicle for this process, asking reflective questions such as, 'did it work?' 'how am I doing?' and 'does it make sense?' (Wertsch, 1978).

Methods and methodology

At the outset of the study I visited a nursery to observe how teachers interacted with children, verbally and non-verbally, to create meaning in planned teaching situations.. A case study approach was appropriate in realising such aims, with non-participant observation as the main research tool. The ability to capture the 'wholeness' of the adult-child interaction was important: as some aspects of interest to the study involved non-verbal techniques, videotape, rather than audiotape, was used. A range of planned activities was observed, three activities per practitioner which were recorded for fifteen minutes duration each.

The first level of analysis was quantitative, where types of interactions and their frequency were identified. Drawing on the relevant literature, I developed a 'start list' of codes which I used to organise the data into groups, according to the 'types' of interaction I observed. These 'types' related to written descriptors for techniques within adult interaction, involving both verbal and non-verbal communication with children in planned teaching situations. Eleven codes were developed: labelling; attributed and simple descriptions; recall and narration; higher order thinking questions; 'testing' questions; rhetorical questions; questions requiring yes/no answers; tag questions; questions which offer children an alternative; narrow questions; broad questions.

Verbal interactions from the videotapes were transcribed in full, for ease of analysis, using an observation schedule and information on non-verbal techniques was added in preparation for coding (see Figure 14.1).

Figure 14.1: Extract from Transcript prepared for Coding Data

Practitioner: Dawn **Activity**: painting   **Time of day**: morning

Size of group: 1-2 **Time period**: 15 minutes   **Adult directed**

Tape starts about 5 minutes into the activity-2 girls are painting, Lydia and Grace; Dawn is sitting with them at the table in the messy room.

Codes	Adult talk/non-verbal actions
	Dawn-Oh Lydia, that's interesting.
	(no response)
activity.	Managerial type interruption from child not involved with
	Dawn-Hmm! (to Lydia)
	Grace-I'm going to do another one after this one.
	(no response from Dawn)
	Dawn-It looks really lovely in the palette (pointing) cos its sparkly. Which one did you use Lydia?
	Lydia (pointing) that one.
	Dawn-This one (picking up a tub of powder paint and examining it)? It doesn't look sparkly in there does it?
	Lydia shakes head.
	Grace-inaudible.
	Dawn (shakes head and looks puzzled, shows paint pot to Grace) I wonder why it isn't sparkly in there then?
	Grace-inaudible
	Dawn (nods) may be if we put water in it'll be full of sparkles?
	Children continue painting Dawn watches them-3 seconds.
	Grace-inaudible
	Dawn-Your mummy doesn't like orange? Do you mean oranges to eat or the orange colour?
	Grace-orange colour.
	Dawn-Does she like oranges to eat?
	Grace-yeah!
	Pause-1 second
	Dawn-I like the colour orange.
	(No response)
	Grace holds up finished painting, moves towards storage area for wet paintings.
	Dawn-inaudible
	Dawn-don't forget your washing up, will you?
	Grace-inaudible
	Dawn (nodding) oh yeah!

Each interaction was then coded giving the frequency of each type of interaction, which group and which practitioner. Throughout the analytical process, any newly identified interaction types were added to the schedule and any not seen at all were eliminated.

During this process, research questions continued to be developed and refined, as did descriptors, when more interactions were revealed and others became more transparent. After analysis of one observation per practitioner, I developed an overview of the types of interactions used by each of them to support children's acquisition of thinking skills. However, this alone would not reveal the concepts of meaning I had sought and become aware of when analysing the transcripts. The frequency of interactions did not reveal the *story* within the learning and teaching episodes. More detailed analysis was needed to identify themes and to show how such themes interrelated.

The typed transcripts of video data and their hand-written codes were transferred to a table designed for more detailed analysis, through the inclusion of a column labelled 'remarks' (Miles and Huberman, 1994). My reactions to what I saw were recorded in this column, together with new interpretations generated as I continued the analysis. General commentary of a reflective nature, resonant with my research questions, was added at the bottom of each page. Additional memoranda recorded emerging concepts so that they could be tested within the analysis of transcripts of other observations. Ultimately, a process of going back and forth through the transcripts evolved, following 'threads' of understanding.

I carried out this detailed level of analysis with two of the original four participants, Dawn, the head teacher and Wendy, the student teacher. Practitioner perspectives were also sought and compared to my developing analysis, noting areas of agreement and dissent.

Practitioners supporting children's thinking skills

Conversation, open-ended questions and thinking out loud are important tools in ... challenging thinking. (DfEE/QCA, 2000 p23)

Both practitioners guided the children's attempts to solve problems through structuring the situation, a characteristic of guided participation identified by Rogoff (1990). This process is initiated in different ways, according to the level of control the adult is taking in the process. The first extract starts when the adult is in control, directing the children to look for minibeasts. In these situations, Wood (1986) recommends that the first step of scaffolding needs to orientate the children to the task so that they are working within the practitioner's goals. In what follows, Dawn attempts to do this through the use of a question,

> Dawn: Where will they be then, do you think?
>
> Children: no response.

This strategy is only moderately successful on its own; in response, some children start searching for minibeasts, others wait and then followed the lead of their friends. Later, Dawn sensed a lull in Peter's activity so attempts to re-orientate him to the task. This time, she uses a statement instead of a question,

> Dawn: If you feel under there you might find a snail (feeling under the leaves).
>
> Peter: no response.

Successful interaction with the child is once again elusive. So Dawn once more changes tack and produces a snail herself, for Peter. This action is accompanied only by an exclamation, with no commentary or questioning,

> Dawn: Ah! (She produces a snail and puts it on her hand showing it to the children and then gives it to Peter).
>
> Peter talks about snails.
>
> Dawn adopts a puzzled expression, intently listening, tilting head to mirror head movement of child.
>
> This continues for eleven seconds.

Vignettes such as these illustrate the different ways in which Dawn attempts to involve the children in her learning goals for the activity, the most effective in this example being action rather than talk. This open-ended strategy is highly successful; Peter talks for eleven seconds. The enabling power of adults' actions is demonstrated further when Wendy, the student teacher, quietly arranges a paper track with blocks placed at intersections, trays of coloured paint, washing bowls full of soapy water and towels. Immediately the interest of the children is captured and a queue forms to take part in the activity.

Scaffolding can only take place when the child, not the adult, initiates the activity. Wood (1986) has identified that the first step for the adult is to assess the intentions of the child. At first, this might seem a straight-forward matter of questioning the child about their play but Tizard et al (1982) suggest that this strategy '... is an ineffective way of eliciting res-ponses, questions and spontaneous talk from the child' (p115). Wendy does not use this approach. Instead, she joins the children at the writing centre and slots into the role of assisting Christopher with a task he has set himself, initiated through the use of a question, not focused on what he is doing but offering support:

> Wendy: Do you want me to give you a hand with those?
>
> Christopher: Yes.

Support is accepted by the child but his intentions do not seem to be established by the adult.

In another example, Rosie, who is playing in the sand, declares her intentions and Dawn offers her support, after clarifying what Rosie's intentions are:

> Rosie: Going to put all the nice shells in here (indicating the yellow mould).
>
> Dawn: Ok, would you like me to help you?
>
> Rosie: (nods)
>
> Dawn: When you said 'nice shells' does that mean all the shells or just special shells?
>
> Rosie: Special shells.
>
> Dawn: How will I know which ones are special shells?
>
> Rosie: Different colours.
>
> Dawn: Oh, right. Is this one (indicating a shell) a special shell?
>
> Rosie: (nods)

All the adult's questions are cognitive demands and the child's thinking is being challenged, yet the contrast with earlier vignettes, in terms of response from the child, is marked. The difference is that the child herself initiates the dialogue, so her interest is established and has only to be maintained. Capturing the interest of the child is crucial to the success of cognitive demands.

Once the child is interested, the adult is able to proceed, providing support with tasks which are just beyond the child's capabilities. Bruner (1986), Wood (1986) and Rogoff (1990) have identified some of the characteristics of these forms of support: simplifying the task, highlighting critical features of the task, instructing, demonstrating, controlling frustration, making connections between what is known and what is new and transferring responsibility for the task to the child.

The following vignettes demonstrate some of the mechanisms Dawn uses to support children:

> Dawn: (watching Rosie scooping sand with two sticks)
>
> Dawn: (reaching across to the shelf for a small plastic tea strainer) Oh have you seen this?

> Rosie: (no response) (reaches for the tea strainer and starts scooping sand into it with a stick)

A short time later:

> Dawn has a large sieve in her hand from the shelf next to the sand tray.
>
> Dawn: (indicating the sieve) Do you want some help? It's not easy to use a stick to pick up sand.
>
> Rosie: (reaches and takes the sieve off Dawn and uses it in the same way she did the tea strainer).

On the first occasion, the adult offers support by suggesting a resource to make the task more manageable for the child. Rosie accepts this, but she continues to struggle with the task she has set herself. Struggle, in this context, provides an opportunity for the adult to recognise that the child is operating within her zone of proximal development (Vygotsky, 1978) and to offer additional support. Dawn offers this in the form of a different resource, which the child finds more successful. Each time, the resource is offered through the use of a question, rather than an instruction. Dawn justifies her questioning approach, in terms of the thinking it encourages from the child, when she reflects:

> I was trying to allow the children to consider ideas by offering choices for the children to make decisions about. Every time the children have to make a decision, thinking skills are employed.

Again, 'yes/no' questions are being used to involve children in decision-making. This final example clearly illustrates Mercer's (1995) point that support commences when the adult defines the task:

> Rosie: I know something (goes round to shelf)
>
> Dawn: There might be something better over there
>
> Rosie brings a mould to the sand tray
>
> Dawn watches Rosie, chin on hand
>
> Rosie puts sieve in mould and tips sand from tea strainer into sieve
>
> Rosie: (inaudible)
>
> Dawn: And it's catching it for us, isn't it?

In this setting, 'defining the task' involves making decisions about the resources to which the children will have free access, to aid them in their self-initiated tasks. Dawn explains,

> Core equipment is provided in the sand that children can rely on. This is indicated when Rosie suddenly looks to the shelf next to the sand tray for the mould – she knows it will be there. Focused resources are added which might be linked to specific children.

Provision of core equipment by the adult that will support the children in their activities is, therefore, an initial part of the process. Analysis of the whole operation, described by the examples above, reveals that first a suggestion is made to make the activity easier for the child: this is adopted. The adult then assesses the child's competence and offers more help, which is taken up, but success is still unattainable. Finally the thinking that 'certain resources will help' transfers to the child and she reaches for something she recalls being available previously. The adult steps back again to monitor progress. This set of ingredients defines the adult support offered within these vignettes. Analysis reveals that individual elements of scaffolding and guided participation exist and that the child is receiving instruction which moves beyond the offer of help. Perhaps the principles of guided participation, constructed from Rogoff's (1990) research into interactions within mother-child dyads in largely American, middle-class homes, do not transfer to the socially and culturally divergent nursery setting in which this research is placed. Alternatively, as Mercer (1995) suggests, it may be too simplistic to compare what parents are able to do with what teachers have to do. Certainly, the findings of this study add weight to the claim that a framework for scaffolding within classroom practice has still to be accurately described (Mercer, 1995).

All four practitioners in the study used talk to generate a social model of thinking. Many of their questions encouraged children to think about what they already knew, rather than demanding the creation of new ideas. Commensurate with findings of Brown and Wragg (1993), where higher order thinking skills are demanded, the headteacher in my study encouraged children to develop a broader range of thinking skills than the student teacher, who confined herself to promoting decision-making. Some of this could be attributed to the two participants' very different levels of experience in working with young children. Children's existing knowledge and ideas were elicited through the use of cognitive demands but when these were not clearly articulated, children were not often pressed to think again, for example, by the use of 'scaffolded' questioning. This may perhaps be linked to the finding that practitioners use statements to generate thinking as well as questions. Children's comments are confirmed, elaborated upon and reformulated through the use of statements by adults. The most prolific use of statements involves a running commentary within the activity.

Use of non-verbal communicative devices

Practitioners used actions to take turns in the discourse, a strategy identified in a study of playgroup workers (Wood *et al*, 1980). As in my study, actions were seen to engage the children's interests more effectively than questions. I found that keeping silent was also a well-used strategy, extended silence was effective in creating a space for children to make prolonged contributions, thus providing opportunity for their thinking to be extended.

All four practitioners in this study supported children's problem-solving through structuring their learning in several ways: sometimes talk is used to simplify or elaborate on the requirements of the task and to offer instructions, often non-verbal communicative techniques such as guiding a child's hand are used. Collectively, these turns illustrate for some of the characteristics of scaffolding (Wood and Wood, 1996) and of guided participation (Rogoff, 1990).

Conclusion

A small-scale study such as this cannot draw generalised conclusions but can be used by others to reflect on their own practices. In doing so practitioners, especially those new to the field may wish to reflect on how they could develop and use their questioning skills to support children's thinking. The importance of observation, being silent and asking the right kind of question at the right point are demonstrated in the examples in this chapter. The development of contingent support for children's learning presents particular challenges for student teachers, not least in organising and managing the task. The role of more experienced practitioners, working in partnership with initial teacher education, needs to be considered to support the acquisition of such skills.

References

Blunkett, D. (2000)The reforms that are pushing pupils up the learning curve, *The Sunday Times,* July 16 2000, p19

Brown, G. and Wragg, E. C. (1993) *Questioning,* London: Routledge

Bruner, J. (1986) *Actual Minds, Possible Worlds,* Cambridge, MA: Harvard University Press

DfEE/QCA (2000) *Curriculum Guidance for the Foundation Stage, London:* DfEE/QCA

Fisher, R. (1998) *Teaching Thinking Philosophical Enquiry in the Classroom,* London: Cassell

McGuiness, C. (1999) *From Thinking Skills to Thinking Classrooms, DfEE Research Report No. 115,* Belfast: Queen's University (ONLINE-http://www.dfee.gov.uk/research/report115.html)

Mercer, N. (1994) 'Neo-Vygotskian Theory and Classroom Education', in Stierer, B and Maybin, J. (eds.) *Language, Literacy and Learning in Educational Practice,* Clevedon: Multilingual Matters Ltd

Mercer, N. (1995) *The Guided Construction of Knowledge, talk amongst teachers and learners*, Clevedon: Multilingual Matters Ltd

Miles, M.B. and Huberman, A.M. (1994) *Qualitative Data Analysis,* (second edition), London: Sage Publications

Rogoff, B. (1990) *Apprenticeship in thinking*, Oxford: Oxford University Press

Tizard, B., Hughes, M., Pinkerton, G. and Carmichael, H. (1982) 'Adults cognitive demands at home and at nursery school', *Journal of Child Psychology and Psychiatry*, 23, pp.105-116.

Vygotsky, L.S. (1962) *Thought and Language*, Cambridge, Mass: MIT Press

Vygotsky, L.S. (1978) *Mind in Society*, Cambridge, MA: Harvard University Press

Wertsch, J.V. (1978) 'Adult-child interaction and the routes of metacognition', *Quarterly Newsletter of the Institute for Comparative Human Development*, vol. 2, pp.15-18.

Wood, D. (1986) Aspects of Teaching and Learning, in Woodhead, M., Faulkner, D. and Littleton, K. (eds.) (1998) *Cultural Worlds of Early Childhood*, London: Routledge

Wood, D. and Wood, H. (1996) 'Vygotsky, Tutoring and Learning', *Oxford Review of Education,* vol. 22, no.1, pp.5-16

Wood, D., McMahon, L. and Cranston, Y. (1980) *Working with Under Fives*, London: Grant McIntyre

Wood, H. A. and Wood, D. J. (1983) 'Questioning the Pre-School Child', *Educational Review* 35, Special Issue (15) pp.149-62

15

Re-thinking reflective practice in the Early Years

Di Chilvers

> For example, when you're with a group you feel like you don't know some things, because you're not an expert, and someone else helps you and that way you learn stuff, like building walls, and the thing you learned sticks inside and it never comes off because it sticks to the other ideas you've already got. Francesco Age 5 (Giudici *et al,* 2001 p326)

Francesco attends a pre-school in Reggio Emilia in Northern Italy; he is involved in a conversation with his peers who are five and six year olds and his teachers about learning groups and group learning. As they talk together, they reflect on their ideas and thinking.

He captures the fundamental feeling of reflective practice very well. His words are accurate and appropriate in that they express what reflection means in the context of teaching young children in early childhood settings. This chapter is concerned with reflective practice in the early years with early years' practitioners. It re-examines reflective practice and how it relates to work with young children, from the practitioners' perspective, whilst offering a model for reflective practice, based on the Reggio Emilia early years philosophy.

Making reflective practice visible in the early years is part of the search. It is a translation of theory into practice. Frequently, theory gets lost when put into practice, if indeed it is ever put into practice. For example, practitioners may learn about new examples of theory, such as reading with real books or emergent writing but they may lack the knowledge, confidence or training to put it into practice.

A study tour in April 1999 to the small town of Reggio Emilia in Northern Italy had a profound effect on my thinking, especially in relation to reflective practice. Here was a model of pedagogy and practice, which was built on 'collaborative reflection' (New, 1994, p35) with young children and practitioners in the infant-toddler centres and the pre-schools, where pedagogy and practice were an integral part of each other. This model was worthy of more exploration, in order to examine practice and philosophy as it relates to reflection. Like Francesco, the things I learned about in Reggio have 'stuck to the other ideas' I already had (Giudici *et al*, 2001 p326). Some ideas have completely altered whilst others have been trimmed and modified to accommodate new thinking, which is still happening years later. This led to further research and dialogue with early years practitioners and students on a B.A. Hons in Early Childhood Studies, to explore their understanding of reflective practice and the kind of 'tools' required for the task.

Methodology – the research process
Research methods should be meaningful, multi-faceted and include a practical element, which is of benefit to the researcher as well as others. The actual 'doing' of the research should be of value as well as the 'end product' for all those involved and it should be seen as a meaningful, stimulating process, rather than a chore. It was essential that the methodology was uncomplicated and unambiguous.

Grounded theory
Grounded theory as a method is open-ended and less prescriptive than others, which allows for a more creative approach to research and one in which the researcher can develop a 'new way of thinking about their research and about the world' (Charmaz, 2000:512). As a 'tool' for research this open-ended, reflexive method can be quite challenging and full of surprises. It can lead to emerging theory which excites and motivates the researcher with unexpected findings, or to insecurity and a loss of confidence because it is so uncertain in its outcomes. Grounded theory requires confidence and trust in ones own thinking and judgement and in other participants contributing to the data collection. Bolton (2001) talks of 'uncertainty' in relation to reflective practice, but this 'uncertainty' is also relevant to grounded theory,

> Reflective practice entails an embracing of: uncertainty as to what we are doing and where we are going; confidence to search for something when we have no idea what it is; the letting go of the security blanket

> of needing answers. This kind of work will lead to more searching ques-
> tions, the opening of fascinating avenues to explore, but few secure
> answers. (Bolton, 2001 p15)

It is the 'searching questions' and the 'fascinating avenues to explore', as well as the idea of emergent theory, which make the use of grounded theory as a method so attractive in this study. The importance of finding out what other people think about reflective practice and not having pre-conceived ideas about it was uppermost, as well as the need to clarify my own thinking, which was uncertain and 'messy'.

Focus groups

The focus group provides a flexible approach to research and allows the voices and opinions of all those involved to be heard. There will be many viewpoints, which need to be respected, as well as the contribution of experiences, feelings, beliefs and attitudes. This research method is collaborative, and enables the researcher to gain other perspectives and clarify personal thinking.

Nutbrown describes her observations with a focus group of five women, illustrating the unpredictability of the method very well,

> One comment – one spoken thought – stimulated another and as the
> conversation went on a verbal sculpture was created, ideas were
> crafted, expressed and re-expressed as each one drew on memories of
> her childhood. (Nutbrown, 2002 p143)

Research methods need not be dull, isolating and confined to the world of academics, they can involve those being researched, which makes the whole research experience a more meaningful, collaborative and reci-procal process.

The use of the focus group involves participants in a reflective dialogue, as they think about and discuss the issues raised by the researcher, who is also a participant. The focus group becomes the vehicle for reflective dialogue and new ideas and is very similar to the reflective dialogue undertaken by practitioners in Reggio Emilia. It was important to 'throw ideas around' and gain multiple perspectives. What we were doing was reflecting on reflection and attempting to make some sense of how we can become reflective practitioners.

A visual picture of research methodology can often help to clarify think-ing and understanding in what can be a complicated and confusing pro-cess. Table 15.1 provides a visual picture of the methodology in this re-search, which is based on four smaller studies. Each study is analysed, looking for common themes and significant ideas in the research data,

Table 15.1: Diagram of methodology using grounded theory

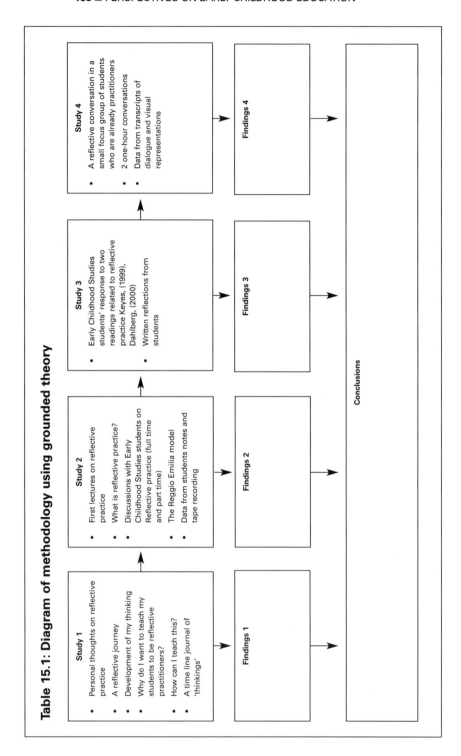

Study 1
- Personal thoughts on reflective practice
- A reflective journey
- Development of my thinking
- Why do I want to teach my students to be reflective practitioners?
- How can I teach this?
- A time line journal of 'thinkings'

Study 2
- First lectures on reflective practice
- What is reflective practice?
- Discussions with Early Childhood Studies students on Reflective practice (full time and part time)
- The Reggio Emilia model
- Data from students notes and tape recording

Study 3
- Early Childhood Studies students' response to two readings related to reflective practice Keyes, (1999), Dahlberg, (2000)
- Written reflections from students

Study 4
- A reflective conversation in a small focus group of students who are already practitioners
- 2 one-hour conversations
- Data from transcripts of dialogue and visual representations

Findings 1

Findings 2

Findings 3

Findings 4

Conclusions

which then form the findings. The findings from the four studies are then analysed and drawn together in the same way, leading to the conclusions.

The studies each represent an aspect of thinking about reflective practice, providing different views and recording data in various ways. Though independent of each other, the studies have connections, which have arisen out of my thinking, the participants' thinking, and the 'knock on' effect of each piece of data: for example, findings from study two and three had an effect on study four.

What is reflective practice?

Being involved in reflective practice is quite a complicated business. There are many views and interpretations of what it entails. Reflective practice does not come in a neat package, but is an inherently messy process, which, as Bolton (2001 p32) substantiates, has no neat or comfortable 'beginning, middle or end'. Other issues arise during the process and confusion and clarity are juggled constantly in a Piagetian process of assimilation and accommodation. Being confused or unsure is all part of the practice of reflection and generates new ideas and thinking. However, in order to understand what reflective practice should look like there is a need to bridge the gap between theory and practice. Both Dewey (1909) and Schön (1987) offer a view of reflective practice but there are also recurring themes which make the act of reflection more transparent and are worth further consideration.

Reflective practice according to Dewey

Dewey, in his prolific, detailed and passionate writings, described a feeling or disposition towards being reflective, rather than an actual physical process. He thought that the practitioner should show 'open-mindedness, responsibility and wholeheartedness' (Pollard, 2002 p17).

Open-mindedness: to challenge ourselves and our own beliefs and assumptions as well as those of others. To be able to listen to all views and take on board all the facts and possibilities. To acknowledge that we may be wrong and take on board others views. To use self reflection

Responsibility: to take responsibility for our own intellectual beliefs and the consequences they may have. Having regard for moral, political and ethical issues and a social awareness

Wholeheartedness: to be enthusiastic, energetic, dedicated, absorbed and single-minded in considering the reflections we make. To ask meaningful and searching questions

(Adapted from Pollard, 2002 p17-18 and Boydston, 1986 p136-138)

These are not the only attitudes required for reflective practice, according to Dewey, but for him they are the 'essential constituents' required for a 'general readiness' (Boydston, 1986 p139) to think reflectively. There are other ingredients in Dewey's translation of reflective practice, which include the art of 'looking', by which he means making observations from which to gather information and details. He describes this 'looking' as 'almost automatic, as an act of research, or inquiry' (*op cit*, p.121), which is undertaken in the immediate context and from which ideas for future action are made. For the early years practitioner today, the act of looking and observing is not a new pedagogical process, but it may not be recognised as being part of reflective practice.

Dewey also emphasised the need for reflection to be a collaborative and interactive process between practitioners in small or large groups, where ideas could be shared and discussed through meaningful dialogue. The emphasis was on the 'shared experiences' and 'co-operative problem solving' (Peters, 1977 p106) of practitioners and definitely not on isolated activity.

Reflective practice according to Schön

Schön's vision of reflective practice creates a metaphorical picture in the mind of the process and readily acknowledges the difficulties of the encounter. He talks of 'high, hard ground overlooking a swamp' (Schön, 1987 p3). Schön describes this 'high, hard ground' as being manageable research with relatively simple solutions, through the use of 'research-based theory and technique' (*ibid*). This would tend to present itself as more scientific, quantitative research. Alternatively, being in the 'swampy lowland' is 'messy, confusing and difficult to solve' (*ibid*) since this is where more 'human' problems are found. Problems or challenges, which are not easily quantifiable, require some careful, complex and sensitive thinking. Schön is, of, course referring to reflective practice, though it is debatable as to how helpful this description is to the practitioner. He goes on to clarify his thinking,

> Shall he remain on the high ground where he can solve relatively unimportant problems according to prevailing standards of rigor, or shall he descend to the swamp of important problems and non-rigorous enquiry (Schön, 1987 p3)

As Dewey described his 'dispositions' for the reflective practitioner, Schön also offers a translation of his proposed theory of reflection. He describes them as a 'sequence of 'moments' in a process of reflection-on-action' (1987 p29). It is helpful to examine Schön's 'sequence of moments', as they contribute to making the practice of reflection visible to the practitioner.

Feeling: to begin with there is a situation to which we bring automatic, spontaneous responses. This is almost an intuitive response, which works so long as it is within the context of a situation. E.g. observing a child parting from their parent and responding appropriately in that situation

Looking: At times there are 'surprises' in the everyday routines. This is an 'unexpected outcome, pleasant or unpleasant' which can lead to exciting and critical moments of interest (e.g. when young children are able to initiate their own learning).

Reflection: Surprise leads to reflection, which can be independent or collaborative, spoken or thought. This is about thinking and considering what has been seen.

Questioning: To enable critical thinking and to set new questions in order to understand what we see and reframe our thinking.

Trying out: Involves testing out our new thinking and our understanding. Are these for the better? There may be more 'surprises', which require further reflection.

(Adapted from Schön, 1987 p28)

Schön sees reflective practice as interactive, with each part of the process feeding in to the other and creating new meanings and 'reconstructing experience' (Schön, 1987 p12), in what becomes a reflective conversation. It is through reflective conversation, with small or large groups, that practitioners can discuss, respond to each other's thinking, agree, disagree, discover and create new ideas and thinking.

This reflective exchange with the situation leads to further framing and reframing for the situation talks back, the practitioner listens, and as he appreciates what he hears, he reframes the situation once again. (Grimmett, 1988 p9)

This kind of reflective practice is evident in Reggio Emilian pedagogy where practitioners are involved in reflective dialogue. It was also evident in the focused conversation groups, which were part of this research.

Reflective practice in Reggio Emilia

In Reggio Emilia reflective practice is made visible by the way in which the early years practitioners integrate reflection in their everyday practice with the children. This is a significant part of the philosophy and pedagogy, which involves a continuous revisiting and friction between theory and practice, where practitioners interpret what they observe and experiment,

...a form of spiralling which allows for taking multiple perspectives, for looping between self-reflection and dialogue, for passing between the

> language of one's professional community (theories and practical wis-
> dom) and one's personal passions, emotions, intuitions and ex-
> periences. (Dahlberg *et al*, 1999 p154)

There is no set order to this process and the same action may be repeated several times in this continuous cycle of 'revisiting and re-representation' (Edwards, 1998:183). In Reggio practice this is part of the project approach which is used with the children. In effect there is continuous dialogue between all those involved in the task.

In Reggio, reflective practice is not spelled out as a recipe to follow but seen as an emerging process which takes on many different qualities depending on how it is used. The feeling is that once a process is made visible by being committed to paper, it is never open to re-invention, ruling out the whole philosophy of questioning, reflecting, dialogue, and constant research. The fact that practitioners can continually question and redefine their practice enables reflection to take place. They are not expected to replicate or regurgitate the same practice continually.

As Dewey identified important dispositions for reflective practice, so do practitioners in Reggio. This is helpful in terms of identifying how reflective practice looks but is not an easy task to put into practice. Rinaldi, the former pedagogical director in Reggio, explains:

> This disposition on the part of Reggio educators to question them-
> selves and then to change their interactions with children based on
> their reflections is behaviour that is valued and encouraged and central
> to their concept of emergent curriculum (Rinaldi, 1992-1993, quoted in
> Hendrick, 1997 p75)

Reggio practitioners have a disposition towards constant learning and on-going development, with opportunities to 'hypothesise experiment, evaluate, reflect and share their understandings with others' (New, 1998 p276). For Reggio practitioners these are the required components of reflective practice, set in a context of collaboration and collegiality. It is through dialogue and collective reflection that meaning and understanding are constructed for a common purpose and practitioners are empowered in their learning and understanding. The support of the group comes from within, where views are made clear so that everyone has learned something and moved on in their thinking. They look for a solution or a next step and arrive at a shared understanding, which either finishes at this point or leads on to other things. A Reggio practitioner voiced her feelings about such collaboration, 'I am convinced that there is some kind of pleasure in trying to agree about how to do things' (New, 1998 p189). This collaborative style of practice has many connections with Dewey's philosophy, in placing learning in meaningful contexts, using dialogue and the joint reconstruction of experience and in the process of open-mindedness, responsibility and wholeheartedness.

The quality of the pedagogy and practice in Reggio is world renowned. Many early years practitioners will recognise and agree with the philosophy, some may even remember a time when they too were involved in discussion and debate to support young children's learning. Drummond acknowledges, 'All young children deserve educators who can take their learning as seriously as this' (Drummond, 1997 p29), and have the time to do so. In Reggio Emilia, an essential ingredient for reflective practice is to slow down. In our hurry to rush children through each stage and on to the next, time becomes a rich commodity. Time, in the English education system is measured in blocks of teaching or hours of learning, but how can they be made quantifiable? In reflective practice there is a need to slow down, stand back and watch, in order to find out what is really happening in children's learning and how we can teach them more effectively.

Throughout the year each Reggio Emilia practitioner is allocated a significant amount of time to engage in collaborative evaluation, research and reflection (Abbott and Nutbrown, 2001 p32), time which is valued as an investment in the development of practitioners' knowledge and skills, and to improve teaching and learning.

One of the principle ways in which reflection is translated into practice in Reggio Emilia is through the use of documentation. Documentation is the tool through which practitioners observe, discuss, and translate children's actions. The documentation may be in the form of written notes whilst watching children, photographs of the development of a project, video footage or slides, children's drawings, paintings and three-dimensional models. This information is used to draw the adults' attention to what is happening and to reflect together on the process, interpret children's thinking and decide what happens next. Vecchi (2001) describes the documentation process as,

> ... to allow us to see and understand better the children and ourselves, as well as to enable others to do the same, so that we can continue to see, reflect, interpret, and understand over time that which took place (Vecci, 2001 p159)

Documentation is the primary means for practitioners to become involved in research and evaluation, which then leads to a deeper understanding of their work with children and of themselves. It is also an important tool for assessment, which respects the way in which children learn and the processes they are involved in, rather than a statistical end

Table 15.2: A framework for reflective practice

Tools	Reflective Practice
Documentation	Gathering together evidence of the children's pictures, paintings, writing, sculpture and words and documenting their learning, usually through photograph, film and display boards. The practitioner reflects on the children's work and together analyses it with colleagues in order to interpret what the children are learning and to anticipate what will happen next.
	It is a 'search for meaning' (Strozzi, 2001:79) and a valuable resource for recalling and reflecting
Pedagogista	The role of the pedagogista 'Is the match that keeps the fire of the Reggio approach lit, constantly prodding teachers to explore different perspectives, to rethink situations, to revisit experiences to be reflective – to stretch beyond wherever it is that they are at the moment' (Phillips and Bredekamp, 1998:445)
Relationships	Collegial relationships between all those involved, children, staff and parents. Based on a willingness to change and to discuss other points of view, share ideas and collaborate. Strong relationships enable practitioners to discuss, argue and question in a safe context
Partnership	Working in partnership with children, colleagues and parents is crucial to reflective practice and collaborative dialogue. Peer partnerships are necessary in order to promote discussion, dialogue and development (Zay, 1998:7)
Dialogue	A constant reciprocal dialogue between practitioners and with children and parents. Dialogue is seen as a shared experience and fundamental to reflective practice. Dialogue and discussion strengthen 'intellectual autonomy' (Malaguzzi, 1998:88)
Listening	Rinaldi talks about listening at many levels. A 'pedagogy of listening' (Rinaldi, 2001 p80-81 and Moss 2001 p128)
	'Listening creatively to the voices within us, and those without, and responding creatively is effective reflective practice' (Bolton 2001:56).
	Observation of children is seen as a way of listening.
Collaboration	Practitioners collaborate and reflect together – to exchange ideas and thinking, to 'listen' to each other and challenge thinking within a safe and appropriate context. A shared experience is fundamental to the philosophy.
Confidence	As practitioners become more confident they become more reflective – they begin to raise the questions – feeding back what they think and trusting their own beliefs and judgements (Knight 2001:35)

Table 15.2: A framework for reflective practice (continued)

Tools	Reflective Practice
Uncertainty	In reflective practice there are areas of uncertainty or looking for something when you are not sure what it is. Uncertainty is a valuable 'tool' in the sense that you are always ready to learn and are more open to that learning.
Experience	Reflective practice develops through the practitioners experience therefore one supports the other. 'Reflection helps the individual to learn from experience because of the meaningful nature of the inquiry into that experience' (Loughran, 1996:14) Reflective practice includes the development of self-awareness and requires reflexivity
Ethics	The practitioner is in a position of 'power and control' (Dahlberg *et al,* 1999:156) therefore needs to acknowledge respect for the child and that each child is different. The practitioner has to take responsibility for what they do and think, 'Ethics enters in because we must take responsibility for our acts, including every act of observing, and for our choices' (*Ibid*)
Questions	Reflective practice requires the use of questions to reveal meaning and understanding. 'I think that from the questions that others ask you (and those you ask yourself), you improve your understanding of who you are, what you are doing, and why you are doing it' (Gambetti, 2001:123)
Tools	The physical tools for reflective practice include: tape recorders to tape discussions to reflect upon at a later point in time, video cameras, photographs, photocopiers, paper and pens, observations, children's pictures, drawings, paintings, sculptures and models.

product. There are interesting links with the use of Learning Stories in New Zealand (Carr, 2001).

Tools for reflective practice

The pedagogy of the early years' centres in Reggio Emilia provides a model of reflective practice which can enlighten practitioners in their search for understanding. Whilst the essential ingredients or dispositions are embedded in the practice, it is possible to identify them and see how it all fits together.

The framework shown in Table 15.2 is adapted from my understanding of practice in Reggio Emilia and highlights the dispositions or

Table 15.3: Research Findings and Conclusions

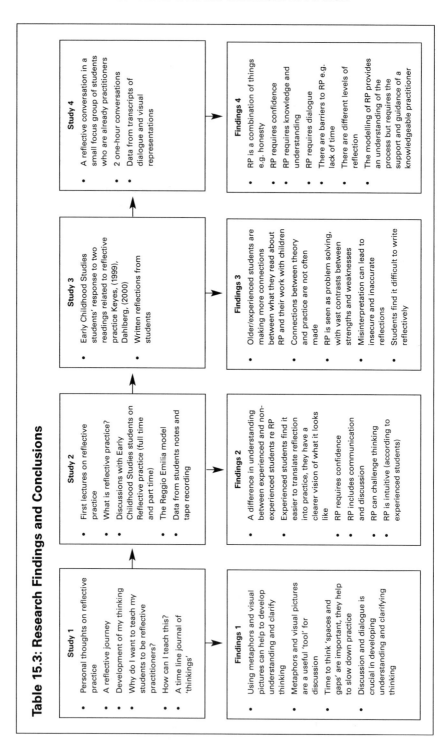

Study 1
- Personal thoughts on reflective practice
- A reflective journey
- Development of my thinking
- Why do I want to teach my students to be reflective practitioners?
- How can I teach this?
- A time line journal of 'thinkings'

Findings 1
- Using metaphors and visual pictures can help to develop understanding and clarify thinking
- Metaphors and visual pictures are a useful 'tool' for discussion
- Time to think 'spaces and gaps' are important, they help to slow down practice
- Discussion and dialogue is crucial in developing understanding and clarifying thinking

Study 2
- First lectures on reflective practice
- What is reflective practice?
- Discussions with Early Childhood Studies students on Reflective practice (full time and part time)
- The Reggio Emilia model
- Data from students notes and tape recording

Findings 2
- A difference in understanding between experienced and non-experienced students re RP
- Experienced students find it easier to translate reflection into practice, they have a clearer vision of what it looks like
- RP requires confidence
- RP includes communication and discussion
- RP can challenge thinking
- RP is intuitive (according to experienced students)

Study 3
- Early Childhood Studies students' response to two readings related to reflective practice Keyes, (1999), Dahlberg, (2000)
- Written reflections from students

Findings 3
- Older/experienced students are making more connections between what they read about RP and their work with children
- Connections between theory and practice are not often made
- RP is seen as problem solving, with vast contrasts between strengths and weaknesses
- Misinterpretation can lead to insecure and inaccurate reflections
- Students find it difficult to write reflectively

Study 4
- A reflective conversation in a small focus group of students who are already practitioners
- 2 one-hour conversations
- Data from transcripts of dialogue and visual representations

Findings 4
- RP is a combination of things e.g. honesty
- RP requires confidence
- RP requires knowledge and understanding
- RP requires dialogue
- There are barriers to RP e.g. lack of time
- There are different levels of reflection
- The modelling of RP provides an understanding of the process but requires the support and guidance of a knowledgeable practitioner

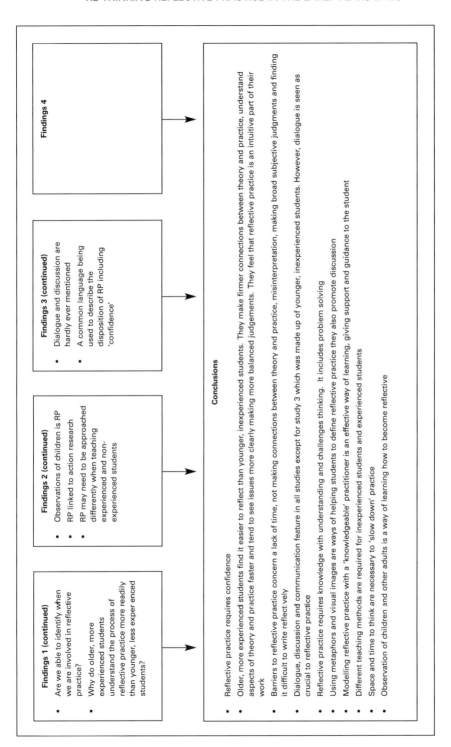

Findings 1 (continued)

- Are we able to identify when we are involved in reflective practice?

- Why do older, more experienced students understand the process of reflective practice more readily than younger, less experienced students?

Findings 2 (continued)

- Observations of children is RP
- RP linked to action research
- RP may need to be approached differently when teaching experienced and non-experienced students

Findings 3 (continued)

- Dialogue and discussion are hardly ever mentioned
- A common language being used to describe the disposition of RP including 'confidence'

Findings 4

Conclusions

- Reflective practice requires confidence

- Older, more experienced students find it easier to reflect than younger, inexperienced students. They make firmer connections between theory and practice, understand aspects of theory and practice faster and tend to see issues more clearly making more balanced judgements. They feel that reflective practice is an intuitive part of their work

- Barriers to reflective practice concern a lack of time, not making connections between theory and practice, misinterpretation, making broad subjective judgments and finding it difficult to write reflect vely

- Dialogue, discussion and communication feature in all studies except for study 3 which was made up of younger, inexperienced students. However, dialogue is seen as crucial to reflective practice

- Reflective practice requires knowledge with understanding and challenges thinking. It includes problem solving

- Using metaphors and visual images are ways of helping students to define reflective practice they also promote discussion

- Modelling reflective practice with a 'knowledgeable' practitioner is an effective way of learning, giving support and guidance to the student

- Different teaching methods are required for inexperienced students and experienced students

- Space and time to think are necessary to 'slow down' practice

- Observation of children and other adults is a way of learning how to become reflective

'important tools' (Moss, 2001 p129) which are required for reflective practice in this model.

Reflective practice in this study

Using grounded theory as a research method requires the careful process of 'sifting and sorting' the emerging data, looking for common threads and patterns in thinking. The four smaller studies led to more emerging thoughts and ideas about reflective practice, which was then drawn together to produce ten points or 'tools' for developing reflective practice, especially during the training of practitioners. (Table 15.3)

The result is a collection of findings which will nurture reflective practitioners in early years settings. Five of the findings discussed below emerged from a process of reflection involving early years' practitioners and students, who have a fundamental role to play in reflective practice.

Nurturing the reflective practitioner
1. *Confidence*
Confidence was important to the students in helping them to interpret what they saw and to put effective pedagogy into practice. There was a clear message that part of nurturing a reflective practitioner involved developing confidence and enabling them to make sense of what they saw. The difficulty is that confidence takes time to develop, usually through experience and maturity. However, if we follow Duckworth's (1987) and Hunt's (1997) approach and engage the students in reflective practice as soon as possible, their experience and understanding will develop and their confidence will increase.

2. *Experience and maturity*
Older, more experienced students found it easier to reflect on their practice than younger inexperienced students. Whilst experience and maturity are extremely valuable, can those qualities be transferred to younger, less experienced students? Schön's (1987) thinking may help here. His view was that students could not be taught to be reflective but that they could be 'coached'. Therefore, for young inexperienced students, the best way of learning to be reflective is to engage in reflection with someone who can support them in this learning and can model reflective practice, as is the case in Reggio Emilia pedagogy.

3. *Dialogue and Discussion*
If we are to nurture reflective practitioners, the students themselves need to be involved in reflection, with plenty of opportunities for dialogue and discussion, to develop understanding and clarify thinking.

4. *Knowledge and understanding*

Students said that reflective practice required knowledge with understanding and ways in which this can be applied to practice. They need to make the links between theory and practice and see the subtleties of reflection, rather than making huge generalisations between what is good and what is not. Dialogue and discussion will develop knowledge and understanding, as well as being involved directly in the practice of reflection. There is a need for opportunities to challenge thinking and to test out new ideas in a supportive group.

5. *Clear interpretation*

Reflective practice is a difficult concept to grasp but requires those involved to have a clear understanding of the process. Lack of understanding was found to be a major barrier and simple and effective teaching methods are required to enable students to engage fully in reflective practice. One such method of teaching is the use of metaphors and visual images, or pictures in the mind. This helps to clarify meaning and to provide a starting point for discussion. Interpretation and understanding cannot be hurried and require time and space to assimilate and accommodate thinking.

What makes these conclusions so valuable is that they came directly from students, who will become, or already are, reflective practitioners. These are the 'dispositions' or 'tools' they have identified as being crucial to fully understanding the process of reflection. Some of these correspond with the 'tools' for reflective practice used in Reggio Emilia pedagogy (see Table 15.2), which shows the similarities between the two approaches.

If connections are made with the Reggio Emilia model of reflective practice, we can devise an approach to nurturing reflective thinkers which is appropriate and meaningful for our own practice. In sharing this model and the 'tools' and 'dispositions' which need to be acquired, early years practice is strengthened and a 'better way of thinking' (Dewey, 1909 p113) is developed for practitioners. To take Malaguzzi's view of the child having 'one hundred languages', what emerges from this study, in collaboration with students, is the beginning of 'one hundred languages' for the early years practitioner, and the reminder that 'if at the end, any message is still needed, it is a message of reflection' (Malaguzzi, 1998).

References

Abbott, L and Nutbrown, C. (2001) (eds) *Experiencing Reggio Emilia implications for pre-school provision*, Buckingham: Open University Press

Bolton, G. (2001) *Reflective Practice Writing and professional development* London: Paul Chapman Publishing Ltd

Boydston, J. A. (1986) *John Dewey The Later Works, 1925-1953. Volume 8:1933* Southern Illinois University Press

Carr, M. (2001) *Assessment in Early Childhood Settings: Learning Stories* London: Paul Chapman Publishing Ltd

Charmaz, K. (2000) Grounded Theory Objectivist and Constructivist Methods in Denzin.N.K, Lincoln.Y.S (Ed) (2nd Ed) *Handbook of Qualitative Research* London: Sage Publications

Dahlberg, G. (2000) Everything is a beginning and everything is dangerous: some reflections on the Reggio Emilia experience. In Penn, H. (ed.) *Early childhood Services: theory, policy and practice* Buckingham: Open university Press

Dahlberg, G. Moss, P. and Pence, A. (1999) *Beyond Quality in Early Childhood Education and Care: Postmodern Perspectives* London: Falmer Press

Dewey, J. (1909) *How We Think* London: Heath and Company

Drummond, M. J. (1997) A Question of Quality: what sort of educators do our young children deserve? In Gura.P (Ed) *Reflections on Early Education and Care* London: Early Education

Duckworth, E. (1987) in Zeichner, K. and Tabachnick, B. R. Reflections on Reflective Teaching in Solar, J. Craft, A. and Burgess, H. (eds) *Teacher Development: Exploring Our Own Practice* London: Paul Chapman Publishing Ltd

Edwards, C. (1998) Partner, Nurturer, and Guide: The Role of the Teacher in Edwards.C, Gandini.L and Forman.G (Eds) *The Hundred Languages of Children: The Reggio Emilia Approach-Advanced Reflections* London:Ablex Publishing Corporation

Gambetti, A. (2001) Conversation with a Group of Teachers in Giudici.C, Rinaldi.C and Krechevsky.M (Eds) *Making Learning Visible: Children as Individual and Group Learners* Italy: Reggio Children

Giudici, C., Rinaldi, C. and Krechevsky.M (2001) (Eds) *Making Learning Visible: Children as Individual and Group Learners* Italy: Reggio Children

Grimmett, P. P. (1988) The Nature of Reflection and Schön's Conception in Perspective in Grimmett, P. P and Erickson, G. L *Reflection in Teacher Education* London: Teachers College Press

Hendrick, J. (1997) (Ed) *First Steps Toward Teaching the Reggio Way* New Jersey: Merrill

Hunt, C. (1997) *Shadows in the swamp: dialogues in reflective practice* pp.1-7 27th Annual SCUTREA conference proceedings 1997 (http://www.leeds.ac.uk/educol/documents/000000247.html)

Keyes, C. (1999) The Early Childhood Teacher's Voice in the Research Community Paper presented at the Third Warwick International Early Tears conference, April 1999

Knight, C. (2001) Quality and the role of the pedagogista in Abbott.L and Nutbrown.C (Eds) *Experiencing Reggio Emilia: Implications for pre-school practice* Buckingham: Open University Press

Loughran, J. (1996) *Developing Reflective Practice: Learning about Teaching and Learning through Modelling* London: Falmer Press

Malaguzzi, L. (1998) History,Ideas, and Basic Philosophy: An Interview with Lella Gandini by Loris Malaguzzi in Edwards.C, Gandini.L and Forman.G (Eds) *The Hundred Languages of Children: The Reggio Emilia Approach-Advanced Reflections* London: Ablex Publishing Corporation

Moss, P. (2001) The Otherness of Reggio in Abbott.L and Nutbrown.C *Experiencing Reggio Emilia: implications for pre-school provision* Buckingham: Open University Press

New, R. (1994) Culture, child development and DAP: An expanded role of teachers as collaborative researchers'. In B. Mallory and R. New (eds) *Diversity and developmentally appropriate practices: Challenges for early childhood education* (p65-83), New York: Teachers College Press

New, R. S. (1998) Theory and Praxis in Reggio Emilia: They Know What They Are Doing, and Why Malaguzzi in Edwards.C, Gandini.L and Forman.G (Eds) *The Hundred Languages of Children: The Reggio Emilia Approach-Advanced Reflections* London: Ablex Publishing Corporation

Nutbrown, C. (2002) 'Focused Conversations and Focus Groups'. In Clough, P. and Nutbrown, C. (2002) *A Student's Guide to Methodology: Justifying Enquiry* London: Sage

Peters, R. S. (1977) *John Dewey Reconsidered* London: Routledge and Kegan Paul Ltd

Phillips,C. B. and Bredekamp, S. (1998) Reconsidering Early Childhood Education in the United States: Reflections From Our Encounters With Reggio Emilia in Edwards, C., Gandini, L. and Forman, G. (Eds) *The Hundered Languages of Children: The Reggio Emilia Approach-Advanced Reflections* London: Ablex Publishing Corporation

Pollard, A. (2002) *Reflective Teaching: Effective and Evidence-informed Professional Practice* London: Continuum

QCA (2000) *Curriculum Guidance for the Foundation Stage.* London: QCA

Rinaldi, C. (2001) The Courage of Utopia and Documentation and Assessment: What is the Relationship? in Giudici, C. Rinaldi, C. and Krechevsky, M. (Eds) *Making Learning Visible: Children as Individual and Group Learners* Italy: Reggio Children

Schön, D. (1987) *Educating the Reflective Practitioner Toward a New Design for Teaching and Learning in the Professions.* San Francisco: Jossey-Bass Publishers

Strozzi, P. (2001) Daily Life at School: Seeing the Extraordinary in the Ordinary in Giudici, C., Rinaldi, C. and Krechevsky, M. (eds) *Making Learning Visible: Children as Individual and Group Learners* Italy: Reggio Children

Vecchi, V. (2001) The Curiosity to Understand In Guidici, C. Rinaldi, C. and Krechevsky, M. (eds) *Making Learning Visible: Children as Individual and group learners* Italy: Reggio Children

Zay, D. (1998) *Reflection-Practice-Partnership: Questions and Points of Tensions in Conceptualizing European Perspectives* pp.1-24 Paper presented at the European Conference on Educational Research Ljubljana, Slovenia September 1998 (http://www.leeds.ac.uk/educol/documents 000000941.html)

Subject index

Author index